LEADING SCHOOLS I

C000037218

PASTORAL WORK

AND THOSE WHO PRACTISE IT:

ESSAYS IN LEADERSHIP
FOR CHANGING TIMES

Edited by

Hilary Moriarty and Nigel Richardson

Published for the Boarding Schools' Association and the
Headmasters' and Headmistresses' Conference
by John Catt Educational Ltd

2010

First Published 2010

by John Catt Educational Ltd,
12 Deben Mill Business Centre, Old Maltings Approach,
Melton, Woodbridge, Suffolk IP12 1BL
Tel: 01394 389850 Fax: 01394 386893
Email: enquiries@johncatt.com
Website: www.johncatt.com

Opinions expressed in this publication are those of the contributors and are not
necessarily those of the publishers or the sponsors. We cannot accept responsibility
for any errors or omissions.

The Sex Discrimination Act of 1975.

The publishers have taken all reasonable steps to avoid a contravention of Section 38
of the Sex Discrimination Act 1975. However, it should be noted that (save where
there is an express provision to the contrary) where words have been used which
denote the masculine gender only, they shall, pursuant and subject to the said Act, for
the purpose of this publication, be deemed to include the feminine gender
and *vice versa*.

ISBN: 978 1 904 724 803

Set and designed by
John Catt Educational Limited

Printed and bound in Great Britain
by Bell & Bain, Glasgow, Scotland

CONTENTS

About the Contributors

John Baugh was born in Uganda and educated at Aldenham School and St Luke's, Exeter. He played professional football before deciding to do a proper job, and taught at Haileybury before becoming Headmaster of Solefield School, Sevenoaks, (1987-1997); Edge Grove School, Hertfordshire, (1997-2002); and the Dragon School, Oxford, (2002-), which is the UK's largest boarding and day preparatory school, with 850 pupils. He was chairman of the Boarding Schools' Association in 2007.

Kathy Compton trained first as a teacher; then, after a career change, as a nurse. Appointed with her husband to run a boys' boarding house at Plymouth College, she was then asked to start and run the medical centre at the school. She also initiated and ran PSHE at the school and completed her Masters in health education and health promotion. She was then co-opted onto the Royal College of Nursing (RCN) school nurses' forum where she represented independent and boarding school nurses. On completion of her term with the RCN she was appointed as the BSA Nurse Adviser, a role she still fulfils alongside her school nursing job at Plymouth College.

Daniel Cross has been deputy head (staff) at The Perse School, Cambridge, since 2008. He read geography at Exeter University and his first teaching posts were at Kingston Grammar School, Surrey, and University College School in Hampstead. He moved to Cambridge in 1999, first as head of geography and then as head of sixth form. A keen sportsman, he has also recently completed an MEd degree at Cambridge University and is a regular contributor to courses organised by INSET service providers.

Peter de Voil was Headmaster of The English College in Prague from 2004-9, having previously been Headmaster of Frensham Heights for 11 years. He taught first at Wrekin College and then at Uppingham, where he became a housemaster. He spent one year at Milton Academy, Boston, USA, as a Fulbright exchange teacher, and for many summers directed residential English language courses for the Bell Educational Trust in Cambridge. He has also been chairman of the HMC community service committee and of HMC projects in Central and Eastern Europe; an ISI inspector and deputy chairman of the English-Speaking Union in the Czech Republic. He is a governor of St

Christopher School and a member of the Academic Board of the Bell Educational Trust.

Delyth Draper was a boarder and head girl at Penrhos College, North Wales. She began her career as a biology teacher and residential house tutor at Kingswood School, Bath, before moving to Bromsgrove School in Worcestershire, where she was assistant housemistress in a boys' house before running a large boarding house for 13 to 18 year-old girls. She then moved to set up and run a new girls' house at Wellington College, Berkshire, before becoming the pastoral deputy head. She is a course tutor for the BSA and a governor at Rydal Penrhos College in North Wales.

Sue Freestone's path to headship was an unusual one. Having graduated with a first from the Royal Academy of Music in 1976, her first post was that of Director of Music at North Foreland Lodge. She ran music departments for 20 years, with a short break to produce two children. Having completed an MEd in educational management at Bristol University she became Head of Sibford School in Oxfordshire in January 1997. She was chairman of SHMIS in 2002 and moved to the Headship of The King's School Ely in 2004.

John Gibson was born and educated in County Durham. After graduating from Bede College, Durham, he began his career as a PE teacher, also teaching geography – a subject in which he took a degree with the Open University. He joined the staff at Leighton Park School, Reading, in 1986 and became a boarding housemaster a year later. Since 1996 he has been Head of Stoke College in Suffolk. He was Chairman of the Independent Schools Association (ISA) in 2009.

Dr Christopher Greenfield was educated at a state grammar school in south Gloucestershire after attending state infant and primary schools in inner city Bristol. He studied at the universities of Leeds, Michigan State, Bristol and at Corpus Christi College, Cambridge, and was awarded his doctorate in education for citizenship by Bristol University in 1996. He has taught in both state and independent schools in the UK and overseas, and he was Headmaster of Sidcot School (SHMIS) for 11 years until 1997. Since then he has been Principal of the International College at Sherborne (ISA) which is owned by Sherborne School (HMC).

Richard Harman has been Headmaster of Uppingham School since September 2006. He was educated at the King's School, Worcester, and Trinity College,

Cambridge, where he read English. Having spent two years working for an academic publisher, he decided his real vocation was in teaching. After five years at Marlborough teaching English and drama, during which time he also completed his PGCE at Exeter University, he spent 12 years at Eastbourne College. After progressing from head of English to housemaster of a sixth form girls' house and then to being a member of the senior management team, he became Headmaster of Aldenham in September 2000 and thence to Uppingham.

Christopher Hirst was Head of Sedbergh School from 1995-2010, where he introduced coeducation in 2001. A pupil at Merchant Taylors', Northwood, he read history at Trinity Hall, Cambridge, and was briefly in banking in South America (where he represented Chile against New Zealand, only to be bowled by the great Sir Richard Hadlee for a duck). He then taught history and ran the cricket at Radley College from 1972-1985, where he was also a social tutor (boys' housemaster), before spending a decade as Headmaster of Kelly College, Tavistock. Since 2010 he has lived in Pembrokeshire and is a governor of several schools whilst also studying for a PhD on 'The public school chapel during the 1914-18 war' at the University of Wales, Lampeter.

Tim Holgate has spent his whole professional life in education. After 20 years at Marlborough College as a head of department and housemaster, he became Headmaster of Warminster School. He then spent a professionally-rewarding 12 years as the first director of training for the Boarding Schools' Association where he was involved in the development of the national minimum boarding standards and a nationally accredited staff professional development programme. Now semi-retired, he is still busily engaged in training and inspection-related activity in the UK and overseas.

Karl Hopwood is an e-safety expert. He is a member of the UK Council for Child Internet Safety (UKCCIS) and sits on the working groups for better education and public awareness. He currently works for a number of key players in the UK and abroad including the Child Exploitation and Online Protection Centre (CEOP); British Educational and Communications Technology Agency (BECTA); South West Grid for Learning (SWGfL); Childnet International; and a number of local authorities within the UK.

He has worked for several years in the creation of policy and practice in the field of e-safety. His background as a teacher and Headteacher mean that he has particular expertise in working with children and young people – which he continues to do – having completed a number of research projects for different organisations. He has recently been employed by the Egyptian government to help to develop their e-safety strategy. He also works for INSAFE, the coordinating node of the EU safer internet programme and is a consultant for the European Commission on internet safety matters.

Hilary Moriarty is national director of the Boarding Schools' Association. An ex-grammar school girl and graduate of Trinity College, Dublin, and the University of Leicester, she trained in tertiary education. She lectured in colleges of further education before teaching in comprehensive and grammar schools, developing academic and pastoral interests as head of English and head of sixth form. For seven years she was deputy head at Red Maids' School in Bristol, while it was still a boarding school, followed by six years as Headmistress of Bedgebury School, a girls' day and boarding school in Kent which closed in 2006.

Penny Oates has been the Head of two Cambridge pre-prep schools for a total of 16 years and has 25 years' experience of working with very young children and their parents. Her post as Head of the Pelican School (1997-2010) involved starting the school from scratch and thus being responsible for setting the standards for all pastoral and academic matters. She has written a book for parents of young children entitled *How to Talk to Your Child: Solving Problems at Home and at School.*

James Priory has been Headmaster of the Portsmouth Grammar School since 2008, having been successively head of English and head of sixth form there. After reading English at Lincoln College, Oxford, he taught at Bradford Grammar School where, as head of Year 7, he helped to introduce the first girls. He is a member of the editorial board of *Conference & Common Room*, a governor of Highbury FE College in Portsmouth, and chairman of Portsmouth Festivities, a city-wide festival dedicated to young people and the arts.

Dr Nigel Richardson has been co-editor of all the five books published so far in this series. He was Head of The Perse School, Cambridge, (1994-2008) having previously held posts at Uppingham, the Dragon School, Oxford, and the King's School, Macclesfield. An appraiser of Heads and teachers, a governor of several HMC schools and a syndic of the Cambridge University Press, he was also editor of the HMC magazine *Conference & Common Room* from 1999-2002. He has written history books for children and training literature for the Industrial Society. He was chairman of HMC in 2007, and is currently working on a biography of the great Victorian Headmaster, Edward Thring.

Melvyn Roffe is Principal of Wymondham College and immediate past chairman of the Boarding Schools' Association. Educated in Derby, he studied English at the University of York and then trained as a teacher at the University of Durham. His experience of boarding began at Oundle School, where he taught English and drama and, amongst other challenges, helped to found a new girls' boarding house as assistant housemaster. He moved to Monmouth School in 1993, first as head of English and later as director of studies. Headship at Old Swinford Hospital followed between 2001 and 2007. He was a founding member of the DCSF Steering Group for boarding places for vulnerable children.

Nicholas Seward was born in Zambia and raised in Papua New Guinea. He went to Millfield School as a boy before reading aeronautical engineering at Imperial College, and then trained for ordained ministry at Durham, with a Master's thesis on C S Lewis thrown in. A curacy in Canterbury diocese followed, and then six years as chaplain, housemaster and head of theology at Magdalen College School, Oxford. He was appointed Headmaster of Kingham Hill School in September 2008, and has a passion for education in a Christian context.

Dale Wilkins began his interest in boarding as a resident tutor at Norwich School in 1986. His first housemaster became a lifelong mentor, and the junior house matron became his wife! They ran a junior girls' house together at Tettenhall College, before moving to Old Swinford Hospital, a state boarding school, in 1992, where he has been housemaster of both senior and junior boys' houses, director of boarding and currently deputy head. He has been a BSA course tutor for 11 years, a boarding inspector, and he produced the Self-Assessment Manual for the BSA.

Introduction and Overview

Nigel Richardson

This is the fifth volume in the *Leading Schools* series, following on from previous titles which focused on the work of Heads; senior management teams; heads of department and newly-qualified teachers.

The chapters have been written by people in a wide variety of school roles – on the assumption that pastoral work is essentially a team exercise. Some (but by no means all) are written from a Head's viewpoint – but wise Heads know that they cannot do more than a proportion of this work themselves; that they need to trust, and to delegate to, others, and that their own input will all too often centre on the most intractable cases, or those involving at-risk pupils or stressed-out staff. They also know that they rely on those in senior and middle management roles to alert them where such issues arise. As a result, people in those roles need to be aware of the legal and other responsibilities that Heads face in these matters.

The structural way in which the pastoral team is organised varies from school to school. Some schools, especially in the boarding sector, have entirely house-based, cross-age arrangements, apart perhaps from specialist advice on university entry and careers. Others, especially day schools, tend to go more for horizontal groupings of two to three years: perhaps led by heads of section in charge of lower school (Years 7 and 8), middle school (Years 9 to 11) and sixth form (Years 12 and 13). There may also be heads of year as well as a tutor team within those sections.

Both systems have strengths and down-sides. For example, a purely vertical system within geographically-dispersed houses makes it harder for like-minded and able pupils to get together for discussion and debate outside timetabled lessons, whereas a purely horizontal one limits the leadership and pastoral opportunities which senior pupils can experience over younger ones via prefect or mentoring roles. As a result, some schools operate a combination of both systems – perhaps a horizontal one for pastoral work and a vertical one for some games and other school competitions. Despite all this variance, we hope that readers will be able to deduce advice which is useful to them, even if it is drawn from a school with radically different systems to their own.

Meanwhile, there are two important issues which underpin many ideas developed in this book. First, pastoral matters have never been more important in schools. The reasons for this lie in part in the social, legal and other developments described in chapter 1. A variety of constituencies including government (of any political party) and fee-paying parents have vastly increased expectations compared with those of earlier times about the extent and specialism of pastoral provision in, and by, schools.

However, we must resist the temptation to assume that our generation invented pastoral care, or that previous generations were completely indifferent to it. Their pastoral style was different – in keeping with the wider social preoccupations and fashions of their time – and in many schools they had significantly fewer financial resources to devote to it. That said though, the past century has seen huge changes: schools and Heads tend (with individual exceptions!) to be less top-down and more consultative in their dealings with both staff and pupils; corporal punishment has disappeared; there is a comparatively new preoccupation with anti-bullying and child protection strategies.

Schools are much more open to the benefits of specialist counselling, psychological and other input from external agencies and individuals. There have also been huge legislative changes in the areas of child welfare and child protection, since the Children Act 1989 ushered in a new era of pastoral inspection, in addition to the growing work of Ofsted and the Independent Schools' Inspectorate (ISI) in the 1990s and 2000s.

In the education of boys, there is less emphasis on the virtues of the stiff upper-lip, the supreme importance of athleticism and ball-games and military styles of leadership than would have been the case in (for example) the decades leading up to the First World War. Pastoral assumptions in girls' schools reflect the vastly increased opportunities for women in universities and careers, especially in science, business and the law. With the growth of pre-prep provision, the independent sector has had to learn or re-invent a whole new range of pastoral skills

– and in doing so its schools have set something of a benchmark for what parents expect from the schools to which their children progress as they get older.

This fact brings us logically to the second issue. Within the independent sector, our schools are just that: *independent*. This situation has great strengths: it tends to encourage individuality and distinctiveness, even in an age when government legislation, recurring inspection and the importance of public exam results risk making schools much more uniform and narrow in their focus.

Independence also tends to lead to good governance and sound financial management. Each school's destiny, for good or ill, is in its own hands. But the down-side of independence is the risk of isolationism, the mentality of 'we know best, and have nothing to learn from others', backed up by justifications based on overwork; the re-invention of the wheel; the fear of local rivals. The risk of these things tends to be greater when the sector feels under threat, either economically or politically.

In pastoral matters, we too often fail to have an overall view of what independent sector schools do, and should, stand for. My own time in schools (1970-2008) was divided almost exactly 50-50 between day and boarding schools: I taught Oxbridge history candidates *and* seven year-olds (religious studies to the latter with, looking back, an alarmingly low degree of competence). In the course of it, I repeatedly encountered two prevailing areas of ignorance about what others do. They may well be excessively stereotypical in what follows in the next four paragraphs, but I suggest that anyone tempted to feel that I've imagined them should search their conscience: they are not living in the real world.

One prejudice lies in the perception gulf between those teaching younger or older children. Senior schools teachers often feel that the school day for younger children is essentially very short; that young children are essentially uncomplicated, creating few of the disciplinary and pastoral issues that senior schools face; that the curriculum issues are straightforward and that for teachers there is little or no marking at the end of it; even (in extreme cases) that the knowledge and skills required to teach younger children are not especially high; that the cost issues in small schools are simple. If you are tempted towards this view, study chapters 4 and 5 in particular.

Teachers of younger pupils often fail to understand the variety and complexity of what senior schools offer both inside and outside the classroom; the extent to which social and behavioural issues consume vast amounts of teacher time; even the idea (again, at the extremes, and based on a complete failure to understand the complexities ushered in by puberty) that if pupils get into trouble in their senior schools it is because 'they were so happy with us that when they reached their next school, it just couldn't handle them'. No, I'm not inventing it: I've really experienced it. If you are tempted to this view, study, for example, chapter 12.

The other prejudice relates to another perception gap, between those working in day and boarding schools. To many of those working in boarding schools, day-school teachers – and Heads – arrive just before 8.45am and depart soon after 4pm (if only!); nothing happens after school or at the weekend; there is an unhealthy, even rather vulgar, preoccupation with exam results; teachers can't possibly ever 'know' their pupils in the way that boarding schools do, even if they have a mind to do so. It is hard for this group to appreciate either the speed at which, in the day-school day, lessons, games and societies follow hard on the heels of each other with only minimal time for a snatched lunch, or the pressures posed by highly assertive parents, living nearby. Maybe chapters 17 and 18 give a flavour.

It is correspondingly hard, even impossible, for those who have only taught in day schools to understand either the immense rewards that total immersion brings to their boarding counterparts (for example in tutorial encounters out of formal school, or in aesthetic activities such as music in the evenings) or the ceaseless, remorseless pressure and huge term-time workload that boarding implies, especially for those who run, or live in, boarding houses – especially in winters when there is mass illness.

It is hard, too, for day school staff to appreciate why the boarding school holidays tend to be longer; why marketing is such a relentless and complex activity; why prep schools have to be so carefully courted; why you need to have a strong sense of community to thrive in a boarding school; why they are such distinctive centres of excellence. Chapters 6 to 8 may help your understanding.

What does all this have to do with pastoral issues? I will chance my arm with a pair of broad-brush statements to serve as an example of the wider issue which this volume hopes to address. The best boarding schools do pastoral work of unparalleled excellence, from which others can learn much – which is why this book is co-sponsored with HMC by the Boarding Schools' Association.

Yet there are some areas in which boarding schools can draw on the expertise of the best day-schools: for instance, in the Rolls-Royce service which the latter provide on public exam results day, and their expertise in giving UCAS advice. Readers may wish to challenge these statements, based on their own experience, or to provide alternatives, or to think of equivalent issues for junior schools which are more relevant to their own situation.

But my co-editor and I suggest that the wider issue is what is *really* important: that all constituencies within the independent sector – day, boarding, junior and senior – have much to learn from the pastoral experience of others (and indeed from the significant expertise of those working outside it). If this book contributes to that process, it will have been well worthwhile.

Chapter 1

The social and educational context in which we work

Nigel Richardson

Let me take you on a somewhat eccentric journey through the first two decades of life, as seen through the work of six very different writers. The situations they describe are all different, yet all have pastoral implications.

Twenty years ago journalist Libby Purves wrote this description of very young children in an international best-selling book entitled *How NOT to raise a perfect child* (Coronet Books 1991, and various other publishers since):

> A baby or toddler has a cheerful, roundish, uncompromising sort of shape: solid chubby legs seem to go well with an opinionated and practical outlook on life. A toddler's jokes are uproarious; his wishes imperious; his temper is uncontrollable and his actions – as far as he is concerned – totally without consequences. Someone will mop it up. Someone will mend it. We shall buy anuzzer one, Mummy, at the shops. There is no problem so pressing that a hug and a warm drink can't solve it.
>
> Then the child changes shape: everything grows lengthways and slims down. Fat legs turn into long spindly ones … and suddenly your ex-baby has begun to turn large, worried, wondering eyes on the rest of the universe. Why it is raining? Will the mouse ever come alive again if Tibby bites it dead? Will I go to prison if I say a rude word to a policeman?

Secondly, here are some thoughts generously made available to me by a well-known author, but written in her childhood:

My thoughts, by Sarah Gristwood, aged 7:
I sometimes wonder what my mind is like inside, often I fancy that it is like this. I feel as if my mind goes round and round like the earth, and if my lessons make me think hard it begins to spin. In my other class it was getting all stodgy and still and lumpy and rusty. I feel as if there is a ball in my mind and it is divided into pieces – each piece stands for a different mood. The ball turns every now and then and that's what makes me change moods. I have my learning mood, my good-looks mood, my happy mood, my loose-end mood and my grumpy mood, my miserable mood, my thoughtful mood and my planning mood.

At the moment I am writing this I am in my thoughtful mood. When I am in my thoughtful mood I think out my maths and plan stories and poems. When my kitten is in her thoughtful mood she thinks shall I pounce or not, and shall I go to sleep or not. This sort of thing goes on in my own mind too. It is very hard for me to put my thoughts into words.

Thirdly, this famous example of a child of ten, probably of quite limited ability, writing about a cow, and taken from *The Complete Plain Words* by Sir Ernest Gowers (HMSO, 1954):

The cow is a mammal. It has six sides – right, left, an upper and below. At the back it has a tail on which hangs a brush. With this it sends the flies away so that they do not fall into the milk. The head is for the purpose of growing horns and so that the mouth can be somewhere.

The horns are to butt with and the mouth is to moo with. Under the cow hangs the milk. It is arranged for milking. When people milk, the milk comes and there is never an end to the supply. How the cow does it I have not yet realised, but it makes more and more. The cow has a fine sense of smell; one can smell it far away. This is the reason for fresh air in the country.

The man cow is called an ox. It is not a mammal. The cow does not eat much, but what it eats, it eats twice so that it gets enough. When it is hungry it moos, and when it says nothing it is because its inside is all full up with grass…

16

Fourthly, a piece which first appeared in *The Times Educational Supplement* (reproduced here by kind permission of its editor). It was written by a very clever prep school boy of 12 or so (identity unknown) who had been told to write an essay explaining why he had been caught disturbing a lesson as he waved to a friend whilst walking past a classroom door:

> Sir, at 12.35pm on the 15th of May I had just finished my art lesson. I then walked to the boys' exit and proceeded in an easterly direction in order to favour myself with one of the school's excellent lunches, which I may add are moderately priced, giving superb value for money. As you can imagine I was highly elated at the thought of this great experience.
>
> My mind was in disarray when passing your window, where I saw my good friend Mark. For some reason unknown to me, my brain sent a message to my arm, telling it to move in a 45 degree angle, and it ordered my wrist to move backwards and forwards. As you can imagine, I was very embarrassed at this involuntary action, and I can only apologise on behalf of my brain for any trouble which it has caused.
>
> I have had this brain for 12 years and 2 months and it has never done anything so irresponsible before. Sir, the truth of this matter is... I have no excuse...

In the first three pieces, we mostly observed how young people take in and assess information. The fourth introduced an element of reasoning – even manipulation – of the knowledge and skills which the child had by now acquired.

The fifth and sixth writers are much more concerned with the way in which slightly older young people react to the world and those around them.

Housemaster James McConnell's words from his book *Eton: How it works* (Faber and Faber, 1967) speak for themselves. They have been quoted (with a number of variations) by many others since, but this is the original version. The author introduced it by saying: 'Perhaps two or three years after a boy enters Eton, he passes into the... Problem Age... I sometimes feel that I ought to have a standard letter which I would dispatch to all mothers on the 15th birthday of their eldest son. It would go something like this:

Dear Mrs…,

Today is …'s 15th birthday. You'll be glad to hear that he received a nice bundle of envelopes and packages in the post this morning. The cake you ordered has arrived safely and I have given him leave to go home to lunch with you next Sunday.

The real purpose of this letter is to try and prepare you for an imminent change in the relationship between yourself and your son. The affectionate small boy who has quite justifiably been your pride and joy is about to undergo such a transformation that you may well begin to wonder whether you have mothered a monster. The piping treble voice, you will observe, has already begun to crack. The down on his cheeks and chin is stiffening into defiant bristles and there is an angry hue about the blemishes on his skin. Perhaps you have already started to wonder where you have gone wrong and what you have done amiss to deserve this kind of anger. You, who have shown him most affection, will seem to be the butt for his most barbed and unkind remarks. That is because you are still the most important woman in his life, and the most convenient target for his burgeoning masculine aggressiveness.

Do not despair. Ride out the storm. Be firm but affectionate. At this moment when he seems to need you least, he in fact needs you most. Make a stand about the principles you regard as fundamental; give him rope about the less important things. Do not worry too much about his wearing apparel or the length of his hair. Comfort yourself with the knowledge that his present moods are transitory.

If you can do this and stand firm as a rock in the midst of his tempestuous life, the small boy whom you thought you had lost will return to you as a charming young man, well-groomed in appearance and with delightful manners. He will have been well worth waiting for.

Meanwhile, we are both in for one hell of a time!

Finally, if you are tempted to think that this is a boys' only phenomenon, consider this poem (in the style of Byron), devised and kindly passed on to me by Clare Gardom whilst on prefect duty a few years ago at a leading school for girls:

> She walks in trainers, tho' she might
> Admit 'tis nor allow'd, nor wise;
> And all that's best of short and tight
> Define her curves, reveal her thighs:
> Skirts roll'd to that immodest height
> At which the teacher tuts and sighs.
> One hair-tie more, one earring less
> Had half-impair'd that nameless grace
> Which waves in each peroxide tress,
> Or jangles gently round her face;
> While desk-top doodlings express
> How dull, how drear this learning-place.
> And on that cheek, and o'er that brow,
> So subtle, yet so eloquent,
> The lashes black, the tints that glow,
> And tell of breaks with makeup spent,
> A heart turn'd always to her beaux,
> A mind to work indifferent!

No wonder that *The Times* gave an eye-catching title to its editorial (23 September 2009) on growing up: 'Teenagers are God's way of showing you what you put your parents through.'

What might we conclude from this literary sextet? That the first 20 years of human existence represent both a huge learning curve and a time of vast changes in outward personality traits. That the brain is even more complex than we had previously thought. That providing a child or young adult with the intellectual equipment to capitalise on it, and the pastoral equipment with which to handle it happily and responsibly, is a big challenge and an even bigger responsibility – as well as a very great pleasure.

Having defined (or at least provided illustrations of) the characteristics we are dealing with, we need to explain how the demands and expectations on us have changed over time: pastoral work, like most things in education, does not stand still. It has undergone a huge transformation in recent decades, as a result of a mixture of technological advance, social trends, medical advance, legal developments and many other changes. The rest of the chapter covers just some of them; it is by no means exhaustive, and you may well think of things that I have missed.

First, notice one striking thing in James McConnell's introduction: the fact that he talks about the *15th* birthday as a defining time. He was writing nearly 50 years ago; it is often claimed that 50 years before that, some *17* year-olds went into the Great War trenches with still unbroken voices. Teenagers have become on average significantly bigger; according to various newspaper reports the average height of both boys and girls grew by one to one-and-a-half inches between 1970 and 2002, and 15 year-old boys are nine inches taller than they were in 1830.

For many, there have been corresponding increases in weight. Puberty tends to start much earlier in both girls and boys, and it often appears to be a much more rapid process than in the past, with huge physical growth spurts and sometimes a high degree of psychological confusion to match. Many of the disciplinary problems which McConnell's generation first encountered in Year 11 (and mine found in Year 10) now appear in Year 9 or even Year 8.

Lower down the school age-range, children are more worldly-wise, and sometimes more worried by their awareness of aspects of the world around them, than they were in an earlier age when Enid Blyton was required reading up to nine or ten, and life centred on dolls and model railways or Meccano. However, this is controversial territory, and we must beware of portraying (say) the 1950s as a golden age of safety, innocence and uncomplicatedness in which stories always ended happily, there was always jam for tea, and children always did as they were told, whilst believing in Father Christmas until their teens.

However, there seems to be a consensus in society that childhood has become foreshortened, and that a proportion of children are too precocious for their own good. This is one factor which puts an added responsibility on teachers (see chapter 2) to avoid getting drawn into inappropriate relationships with pupils at a time when the widespread use of email, texting and social networking sites is changing the nature of the teacher-pupil relationship.

How has this come about? In part, because of the huge range of information to which young people are now exposed, some of which they may be able to handle intellectually but not necessarily emotionally – or at least, not without careful pastoral guidance from *someone* (of which more later). This in turn stems from the impact of television, advertising and the internet – much of it very beneficial, but some of it manipulative, exploitative and deeply worrying. Children are too often seen purely as consumers in a market.

Meanwhile, over a long period of time, bringing up young people in the broadest sense has become more child-centred. Within the wider family there is less of a hierarchical style: fewer relatives who have to be called 'uncle' or 'aunt'; a greater willingness to explain how adults interact and how the world works. In our predominantly liberal society we have relaxed what can loosely be termed as censorship controls, believing that, on balance, treating children as young adults and not wrapping them up in emotional cotton wool is a laudable philosophy. We have recently become preoccupied with the concept of 'emotional intelligence'; this is a phrase about which I was profoundly sceptical when I first heard it but which, over my years as a Head, I found made increasing pastoral sense.

In schools, education is less top-down than it once was. We concentrate in both assessment and inspection more on learning rather than merely on teaching. We encourage freer discussion of social and ethical questions – which sometimes also means offering explicit factual information (for example, in PSHE), which an earlier generation of teachers would have found deeply embarrassing, even disturbing. There is a less stifling sense of hierarchy here too – and of discipline: we no longer cane pupils and we encourage our prefects to act more as elder-sibling figures than to have the outlook on life that says: 'We suffered, and they'll damn well suffer in their turn.' A greater willingness too, to accept, even to celebrate, individuality rather than to seek to stifle it; we no longer use a ruler or tape measure to calculate the length of hair or the width of trouser bottoms as teachers did when I was at school in the 1960s.

We are more accepting of the child who does not wish to play 'major' school games, or who wants to be absent to represent county, or even country, in an activity which the school does not offer. We offer some new imaginative opportunities for pupils to shine; if you doubt this, think of those who may previously have made little impact within your school but who suddenly inspired a Young Enterprise company. We also ponder more, and rush to judgement less, on the causes of social friction between children; on ethical or religious doubts, and on complex issues of sexual orientation.

And, as an aside, while some of these developments have made the pastoral role of the teacher much more challenging, there may also be an interesting long-term benefit to schools. It can be argued that the independent sector pays a high price these days because too high a proportion of gifted journalists were unhappy in our schools at a time when those schools had more of a strait-jacket mentality (although admittedly when many of them were also far more financially pressed). Maybe this hostility will diminish over time, as we reap the results of having become more varied in co-curricular terms, more tolerant and pastorally empathetic, and more skilled at dealing with divergent skills, and not just with the conformist?

There are many other issues which could appear in this chapter. One involves some future-gazing. With such rapid changes already in off-setting the effects of infertility, will the pastoral teacher of the future have to be prepared to offer guidance on issues of identity to an increasing number of children asking: "Just who am I, exactly?" Other chapters in this book, and in the previous title in this series for NQTs, deal at length with the legal framework in which pastoral work is now conducted. Bullying, child protection, and health and safety legislation all have a major impact on our work. For the most part, this has had a very beneficial effect on the lives of our pupils, although for the pastorally-minded teacher there are residual concerns about (for example) the risks of a false allegation being made against a teacher who gets highly involved pastorally in the affairs of a complex or troubled child. There are also concerns in schools about a parent going to the police, social services or another outside agency before the school has been given the chance to investigate a bullying allegation.

Finally, we need to reflect on the huge social changes which have driven so much of the pastoral development of the past half century: a time when government has looked to schools more and more to do the work which others – including parents, the church and voluntary youth organisations – once did, or which was not previously done at all. The biggest single change has been the fragmentation of the traditional family pattern of working husband plus non-working wife; marriage (once) before children; adults becoming parents in their early to mid 20s. You know the rest. It was never quite as simple as that, of course, but it serves as a useful template.

As all schools know, a rapidly increasing number of children now come from homes with only one parent, with a step-parent or live-in partner, with step-siblings. It is estimated that up to a third of children whose parents divorce will lose contact with one of their parents completely (in practice, usually their father). Day schools deal with the fall-out from families where both parents are working very long hours, sometimes away from the home city. Boarding schools have always had a proportion of children 'sent away' because it was more convenient, and with those who feel pushed out when both parents remarry and both acquire or begin second families. All schools cope with regrettably high numbers of children, one of whose parents dies suddenly and at a young age. They also periodically have to mediate in minor conflict between pupils and parents who are significantly older than their children, either because the parents had children very late in life, or because they have been married or in partnerships more than once, and second time around everyone's standards and expectations are very different.

Stating these facts is not to condemn the often heroic efforts of the single, step, elderly or overworked-and-absent parent. Nor is it to say that such situations automatically cause problems (far from it). Nor to claim that children in more 'conventional' households are always academically motivated and pastorally secure: merely to point to some of the tutorial challenges and demands on a teacher's time which can *sometimes* arise as a result.

Meanwhile parents and children alike live in a society in which the pressures to succeed and to get to the top are much greater than they once were: not least in the fact that good exam results – first time – are the key to a 'good' university, and that the path of retakes is inconvenient and expensive. With A level grade A/B percentages now above 90% for an increasing number of schools, more pupils seem to worry more about standing out or even letting the school down.

What is the end result of this combination of human, social and educational change, the remorseless pressure to succeed, and child-centredness? I suggest that it is a worrying degree of parental anxiety, too much of which gets transmitted to our pupils themselves. Lurid headlines about dangers and risks to children; gloomy headlines about falling educational standards and the need to get straight As (or even more) for entry into some parts of higher education; agony columns in the lifestyle supplements of leading national newspapers about the difficulties of good parenting; news reports about teenage suicide all contribute to a gnawing sense of worry in the current generation of fathers and mothers of young children and teenagers.

They cause some paradoxes too – such as the mother who bought a mobile phone for her son as early as his fifth birthday, yet who still accompanied him every time he needed to answer a call of nature. Again, one must be careful not to see the past through rose-tinted spectacles. Maybe every generation of parents whose children are now in their 20s (which is the situation in which I now find myself) feels this about its successors, but I still believe that over recent years the worry levels have become more pronounced.

Do we under-estimate the importance of helping staff to develop their emotional intelligence, diplomatic and mediation skills? There has been a rapid growth of professional mediation services in other fields, notably in the field of marriage difficulty. Can we learn from it? Do we need training in conflict resolution? Do we train new, young staff sufficiently in how to handle parents' evenings, or how to write letters home to parents? Could we learn from the hotel industry about training in customer care? Are we right to assume that a bright and promising new teacher of 23 or so can *automatically* tackle parents' evenings, sitting across the desk from, for example, a very professionally successful city financier or university don who has much older children from an earlier marriage, and who may be thinking: 'You are young enough to be one of my own children'? Maybe there is a scope for new INSET courses here.

In the end, though, I come back to the ever-fascinating topic of Growing Up: its changes, advances, surprises. Adolescence is a rich source of one-liners for the education profession – not least in reports and references:

> Camilla is a well-formed, attractive young lady, somewhat inclined to pout.
>
> Smith consists of two blobs. The large one underneath is indicative of his sloth and gluttony. The tiny one on the top is said to contain a brain.
>
> X is the youngest of three brothers. Unfortunately the intelligence ran out before the breeding instinct.

The Camillas, Smiths and Xs of the world all present their challenges, and sometimes they make big demands on our pastoral time. I guess we would not have it any other way, because pastoral work can be a source of unique satisfaction to those of us who enjoy it. Even so, there will be bad days, too. Remember the question (allegedly) once overheard in the Dragon School Common Room at report-writing time: "Tell me, how *do* you spell the word Bastard?"

It is the purpose of the chapters which follow to help you to ensure that the bad days are kept to a minimum.

Chapter 2

Pastoral issues and the law

Sue Freestone

One of the supreme joys of headship is that no two days are the same. Every one presents new challenges and fresh problems to be solved. However, the frightening truth is that the areas of life in which we function carry heavy responsibilities, many of which require, at the very least, a working knowledge of the law. Our work on the pastoral front requires that we acquaint ourselves with laws concerning child protection; education; employment; special educational needs; disability and other discriminations, and human rights with regard to religion and the like – to say nothing of certain aspects of marital law and the Data Protection Act.

No Head can be expected to know everything, especially in a world in which new legislation hits us weekly and in an area where the stakes are so high both for our schools' and our own reputations. However, what can be reasonably expected is that a Head should know the basics, and have the wisdom not to act without checking first that his or her toes are not dangling over the abyss. When any issue involving the law, and particularly child protection, hits our inbox or (more likely) our telephone, we are relied upon by our communities to provide informed leadership and to lead with confidence and courage.

We also need to ensure that those in senior and middle management are aware of the legal demands which fall on schools and Heads – and that they play their part to the full in seeing that these are complied with. Not only that, but much of what follows has implications too for the houseparent or tutor or, indeed, anyone carrying out pastoral work with young people.

Child protection

There is no area of headship more fraught with legal pitfalls than that of child protection and all of its associated issues. The first, and arguably most important point I would make is that Heads do not have any choice when it comes to communicating child protection concerns. Myths abound about the discretion we may exercise. The reality is that we have little wriggle room and that message must be conveyed to all of our staff, particularly those with specific pastoral responsibility. Regular training for all teaching staff is essential and child protection training should form part of new staff induction for all who come into any kind of contact with pupils.

Confidentiality

One area worth emphasising here is that of confidentiality. Whenever a child makes a disclosure, it is essential that the teacher or other person to whom it is made makes it absolutely clear, as soon as it becomes possible that anything relating to abuse may be about to be disclosed, that the information will have to be shared. Young, inexperienced staff are particularly vulnerable here, and, of course, they are often the staff to whom pupils most closely relate.

I am frequently amazed, when conducting interviews for new appointments, by the fact that many teachers, even some with many years of experience and already in quite elevated posts, do not know that they cannot try to deal with things unaided and keep a secret when asked to do so by a pupil. I am equally amazed by some who would tell half of their colleagues before thinking to inform the designated child protection officer.

Whilst the need to share information with a member of staff who is trained and experienced to deal with things appropriately is of paramount importance, the need to keep those who know to a minimum comes a close second – in the interests of the child concerned and of damage limitation. It also lessens the dangers of contravening the terms of the Data Protection Act. However, colleagues, at all levels within the organisation, should be aware of the need to inform the Head of the existence of any child protection concern, or any matter that may come to the attention of the police.

Your own understanding of the issues

A good place to start is with the Sexual Offences Act 2003. It is easy to find online (www.opsi.gov.uk/acts/acts2003/ukpga_20030042_en_1) together with copious guidance. It does not make pleasant reading, but it is worth familiarising yourself with the main features, especially those that relate to children. It is important to note that *abuse of a position of trust* relates to all those under 18 and can be reasonably applied to all students in a school which, it goes without saying, should be a place of safety.

All of our employees are in a position of trust, regardless of status – and are wise to assume that this means trust in relation even to pupils (of any age) who have finished taking A levels and are in the process of leaving the school. The entire act relates to pupils of *all* ages as well as staff and other carers and it is a sad fact, worth remembering, that a high percentage of sexual abuse against children is perpetrated by those who are themselves under 18. It is well worth establishing a relationship with your Local Safeguarding Children Board and it is important to know the procedures they have established.

It is beyond the scope of this short chapter to give full details of how you should respond to suspected cases of child abuse, from whatever source, within your school. However, there are many very useful resources on the internet. I commend the child protection section of www.teachernet.gov.uk, which sets out very clearly the structure you should have in place and steps you need to take when the need arises.

Key responsibilities

Within the maintained sector, included within the Head's responsibility is the need to ensure that:

- procedures are in place for handling cases of suspected abuse (including allegations against staff and volunteers), which are consistent with those agreed by the Local Safeguarding Children Board and easily available to all staff and volunteers for reference;

- a nominated governor on child protection issues and school policy be appointed and regularly involved;

- a designated senior person be appointed to coordinate action within the school and liaise with other agencies on suspected abuse cases;

- the designated senior person receive appropriate training and support;

- the role of the designated senior person be fully understood, not least by the Head him/herself;
- all staff know and are alert to signs of possible abuse and know what to do if they have any concerns or suspicions;
- parents are aware of the school's child protection policy;
- the school works with local partners such as Local Education Authorities and Social Services Departments to create a safe environment for children at the school.

e-communications

New implications relating to the internet and e-communications are manifold. Although the act predates the difficulties we face created by the use of the internet and mobile phones, with all of their increasingly elaborate capacities, those uses fall directly under the terms of the act.

The 2003 Act changes the age of those who fall into *the indecent photographs of children* category to all under 18 years of age, (previously the age of 16 applied). It is important to have a policy that deals with abuse of electronic equipment as it relates to invasion of privacy and indecent photography. When considering the dangers of e-communications a visit to the Child Exploitation and Online Protection Centre website, (www.ceop.gov.uk), may be helpful, or to: www.opsi.gov.uk/acts/acts2003/ukpga_20030042_en_1

The duty to share information

As independent Heads of independent schools, we are often tempted to consider ourselves exempt from the strictures applied to our maintained sector colleagues. However, child protection is a prime example of an area in which we can feel, and indeed find ourselves, alone and exposed with very little protection or support.

A good working relationship with social services and the Local Safeguarding Children Board, preferably established before the need arises, can prove invaluable. The new Vetting and Barring Scheme, discussed towards the end of this chapter, which came into force on 12th October 2009, places additional and enforceable obligations on us to share information.

Pupil records

What should be included in educational and curricular records?

However such documents may be labelled within our schools and whether they be kept in houses or centrally and maintained by tutors, housemasters and mistresses or heads of year, what follows must apply.

The curricular record

This must contain a formal record of a pupil's academic achievements and his or her other skills, abilities and progress in school. The Head is responsible for ensuring that a curricular record is kept for every pupil registered at the school and updated at least once every school year.

The educational record

This will include the curricular record together with other information about the pupil that may be kept by the school, such as details of behaviour, health and family background.

A pupil's educational record is made up of any recorded information, other than information which is processed by a teacher solely for the teacher's own use, which:

a) is processed by or on behalf of the Head or a teacher at any school, including reports, grade cards, value added data *etc*;

b) was created by or supplied by the school (or former school) attended by the pupil to whom the record relates, on behalf of any employee, including reports from educational psychologists or other professionals engaged to assess the pupil by the school or the pupil's parent(s);

c) is a statement of special educational needs held in respect of the pupil;

d) is a Personal Education Plan (PEP) held in respect of the pupil. The PEP is the document which provides a record of educational needs, objectives and progress and achievements for children receiving any kind of additional support.

The further information in the educational record will include child protection records where appropriate, records where a child has a statement of SEN and records regarding rewards, sanctions and exclusions.

All records relating to child protection concerns should be kept in a separate, secure and confidential file and should not be included within the pupil's main educational record. If the child changes schools all records and associated concerns should be passed on to the new school.

We have a duty to retain records on pupils: see the Toolkit for schools on the website of the Records Management Society (www.rms-gb.org.uk/resources/848), which is a highly valuable source of advice.

Disclosing educational records

Heads have a duty to disclose a child's educational record to his or her parents within 15 school days of any written request to see them, or to the child him or herself within 40 school days. However, according to the terms of the Education (Pupil Information) (England) Regulations 2005 and the Data Protection Act 1998, **some information must not be disclosed** as follows:

- information, the disclosure of which would be likely to cause serious harm to the physical or mental health or condition of the child or someone else;
- information as to whether the child is or has been subject to or may be at risk of child abuse, where the disclosure of that information would not be in the best interests of the child;
- references supplied to potential employers of the child, any national body concerned with student admissions, another school, an institution of further or higher education, or any other place of education and training;
- information supplied by the school in a report to any juvenile court, where the rules of that court provide that the information or part of it may be withheld from the child;
- information concerning the child, which also relates to another person who can be identified from that information or which identifies another person as the source of that information. Unless the person has consented to the disclosure, or it is reasonable in all the circumstances to disclose the information without his/her consent or the person is an employee of the LA or of the school. (This exemption does not apply

where it is possible to edit the information requested so as to omit the name or any other identifying particulars of that other person.);

• information recorded by the pupil during an examination.

Pupils changing schools

When a pupil is being considered for a place at another school or institution of further or higher education, the educational record must be provided within 15 school days of receipt of the request. Where a pupil is applying to a maintained school, the records sent **must not** include results of any assessments of the pupil's achievements. It is not clear that this restriction applies to pupils from independent schools under consideration.

When a pupil actually leaves one school and becomes registered at another, either maintained or independent anywhere in the UK, the governing body or Head of the old school is responsible for transferring the pupil's educational record to the new school. This must be done no later than 15 school days after the day when the pupil leaves the old school.

Unknown destinations

When a school does not know a pupil's new school, the duty to transfer a pupil's record does not apply, especially when it is not reasonably easy to find out where the pupil has gone. What is considered reasonable will depend on circumstances, but schools might be expected to telephone and write to a pupil's parents. Where neither of these approaches is successful, and it would involve disproportionate effort to discover a pupil's new school by other means, the school will be justified in deciding it is not reasonably practicable to fulfil the requirement.

Although it is not a requirement that they should do so, in these circumstances schools are encouraged to send a transfer file for that pupil, via the School to School (S2S) website, identifying the destination school as unknown. The information is then stored in the Lost Pupil Database. Schools which do not receive transfer files for new pupils can ask the local authority contacts to search this database to see if the files are there.

It is particularly important to go through this process when a child is considered to be vulnerable in any way. One of the potential loopholes we have been guilty of allowing to remain open within the independent sector has been in seeing children leave our schools without ascertaining where they have gone. They are in danger of disappearing off the educational radar and losing a vital source of protection and security.

Health and safety

Together with child protection, our health and safety policies must be reviewed and endorsed by governors on an annual basis. This is one area where checks of our sites and procedures by an outside agency are advisable. Our duty of care to provide a safe environment is a heavy responsibility and it is helpful to have the formal approval of a company that specialises in H&S matters as support in the event of an accident or incident potentially damaging to members of our community or the public. Even if members of the public are on our site without permission, if they hurt themselves it is still our responsibility.

Education

Although education *per se* falls outside the remit of this chapter, we all know that a child's potential to thrive academically is intrinsically bound to his or her emotional and psychological wellbeing. We also know that parents will frequently claim that a child has been bullied or victimised by a teacher when they wish to remove a pupil and avoid paying fees in lieu of notice.

In general terms it is important to have key policies in place and to stick to them. They must be approved by governors and reviewed frequently, always taking account of any changes in legislation. Compliance becomes an ever more pressing issue under the rigours of the new ISI inspection requirements and failure to comply will have far-reaching and expensive consequences.

The ISBA website is an excellent source of model policies, and we should all keep abreast of the valuable briefing material published in the ISC bulletins.

The following list of required policies is by no means exhaustive and will be out-of-date before the ink on my printer has dried. However, for what it is worth, the following may offer a useful starting point. The review periods are the minimum suggested and some changes will be brought about by revised legislation.

Policy	Review Period in Years
Admissions	2
Anti-bullying	2
Attendance and truancy	2
Child protection	1
Crisis management	2
Curriculum	2
Data protection	2
Drugs, alcohol and smoking	2
Disciplinary investigations	2
Educational and physical accessibility	1
Use of electronic equipment	1
Equal opportunities	2
Exclusion	2
Health and safety	1
Internet and email, acceptable use	2
Learning support or special educational needs	2
Pandemic	as guidance develops
Parental complaints	2
Pupil diversity (*ie* anti discrimination)	2
Recruitment and appointment of staff	2
Relationships	2
Remissions	2
Suspension of normal school routines	2
Theft and security	2
Use of reasonable force	2

Appointment of staff

We are all aware of the need for caution in appointing staff and of the new Vetting and Barring system, the first phase of which came into force on 12th October 2009. The second phase, which allows individuals to start applying for registration, applies from 26th July 2010.

Heads will notice the changes from earlier practice set out below. Perhaps the most important from our perspective is that the new legislation places a duty on Heads to share information with the Independent Safeguarding Authority (ISA) when a member of staff is dismissed in connection with child protection concerns or if s/he resigns prior to dismissal. A new offence has been created, punishable by a fine, for employers who fail to provide relevant information to the scheme, without a reasonable excuse. Referral to the ISA will not result in automatic barring. The individual concerned will be given an opportunity to explain his/her actions. Employees include volunteers who may work in our schools.

The new arrangements have been phased in. October 2009 brought changes to the way in which vetting takes place.

- The Protection of Children Act (POCA) list, the Protection of Vulnerable Adults (POVA) list, List 99 and the court-imposed disqualification order regime no longer exists. Instead there is one list of those barred from working with children and a separate, but aligned, list of those barred from working with vulnerable adults.

- Checks take place before an individual is able to start work. The scheme makes sure that those who are known to present a risk of harm to children and/or vulnerable adults cannot enter the relevant workforce in the first place.

- The ISA makes all decisions on who should be placed on the Barred Lists. It does this before an individual is employed.

- When new information, such as a conviction or caution or a referral from an employer, becomes known about an individual already registered with the ISA, the Authority reviews its original decision not to bar. Where an employer has already checked on an employee's status with the ISA, that employer is notified automatically if their employee's status changes.

- The scope of the new Vetting and Barring Scheme is much wider than the former arrangements. It is estimated that around 11 million individuals will have to pass through the ISA checking process in its first five years.

- Once people have registered with the ISA, future employers are able to check their status online and free of charge.

- As with the previous arrangements, Heads have a legal duty to refer relevant information about individuals to the ISA.

- All new employees and volunteers must register with the scheme. The cost for doing so (£64 at the inception of the scheme) includes CRB disclosure. It is free for volunteers. Once an individual is registered they never have to reapply and, in time, the need for CRB checks on new employees will become unnecessary. The cost falls to individual teachers although it is likely that many schools will pay for those currently in their employ.

Further information is available on the ISA website at: www.isa-gov.org.uk

Interviewing candidates
In addition to all these complexities, since 2005 we have had a duty to ensure that at least one person who conducts interviews for new appointments has been trained to probe child protection issues via the Safer Recruitment Programme. From 1st November 2009, Safer Recruitment Training for Schools became a Children's Workforce Development Council (CWDC) programme although, thankfully, those who have already qualified will not need to go through any additional training.

In some schools training has also been undertaken in Warner Interviewing techniques which, although time consuming, can be very revealing and may help to avoid appointing an individual who may not be safe to work with children.

In a chapter of this length, it is possible only to tickle the surface of the legal complexities associated with running a school. For example, I have not even mentioned employees towards whom we have a duty of care equivalent to that we owe our pupils. We also need to have a working knowledge of disciplinary issues, complaints and grievances, discrimination, and if we are unlucky, wrongful dismissal, constructive dismissal, unfair dismissal, redundancy and even Employment Tribunals.

However, there is plenty of advice to be had and the best has to be to keep reading the regular bulletins from the ISI and the HMC Weekly News. In this area of the law, we live in a period of continuous change. Meanwhile, when trouble rears its ugly head, like any good scout: Be Prepared!

The editors are very grateful to Geraldine Elliott of Reynolds Porter Chamberlain LLP for her advice on the legal aspects of this chapter.

Chapter 3

Pastoral strategies, teams and tactics

Tim Holgate

An article in *The Times* (14th July 2009) compared children to dogs and cats. Younger children, it stated, were like dogs – you feed them, train them and boss them around. They come when you call them and regard you enthusiastically and with open affection. Then, at around the age of 13, the adoring little puppy becomes a big old cat. What worked before has the opposite effect. It runs away when called and does precisely what it wants to do. So you have to put food out and let it come to you in its own time. Love and affection are still needed, but on its terms. Negotiation is central to good relations. This amply reminds us of how important it is to consider the age and developmental needs of children and young people when planning for their welfare and providing the resources and strategies for their care.

Pastoral care has been defined in many ways and can mean different things to staff in the many different types of schools in the UK. It can perhaps be considered as the provision of advice and support that young people need for the problems and challenges they face, together with the improvement of the policies and practices that affect their lives. We can thus look at pastoral care from different viewpoints:

(a) The delivery of pastoral care will take place not only on an individual level through formal tutoring or informal contact and advice, but will also occur in groups through tutorial sessions, house meetings, PSHE lessons and the like. There is also the whole-school provision of pastoral care from the point of view of clear expectations and procedures and policies underpinning the work done on an individual and group level.

(b) Pastoral care has been considered to occur on three levels:[1]

- *reactive pastoral care* (referred to as emotional first aid by Hamblin[2]) responds to pupils who present problems of a personal, social, behavioural or emotional nature. It is thus usually provided on a one-to-one basis, and will often involve conflict resolution, behaviour/anger management, or involve staff who are practised in counselling techniques.

- *preventative or pro-active pastoral care* aims to equip pupils to cope when potential crises occur. It will be an integral part of the induction programme for new pupils and tutorial/form periods. It aims to develop practical knowledge, skills, resilience and coping strategies to help pupils to make wise choices and respond positively to challenges.

- *developmental pastoral care* operates at a whole-school and curricular level, responding to the wider needs of the school community, important for pupils' social and personal development, and improving the quality of their lives. It will establish clear expectations for the pupil body, often with their own input, and may involve aspects of citizenship and PSHE. It is holistic and forward-looking, and may involve raising self-esteem or giving pupils opportunities to develop independence and initiative.

(c) Pastoral care provides the opportunity to fulfil the legal duty of care, both by safeguarding pupils through, for example, child protection and anti-bullying procedures, and by promoting their welfare, ensuring that they develop socially, morally, physically, intellectually, emotionally and spiritually, at an appropriate level according to their age.

(d) The provision of pastoral care in school also fits neatly into the realisation of Maslow's five hierarchical levels of need[3] – physical needs, the need for security and safety, the need for a sense of belonging, self-esteem and self-respect, and self-realisation. Pastoral care thus has a large part to play in the achievement of the second, third and fourth of these.

(e) Much of the pastoral care provided by the school will probably occur within the formal structures of the house, form or tutor group, and will involve regular guidance and monitoring from staff given responsibility for particular pupils. However, much valuable pastoral care occurs informally through pupils' contact with many other different adults. Many of these will not be teaching staff, particularly in a boarding school, and pupils may seek out and unburden themselves to supportive people in almost any area of the school.

The importance of pastoral care

Pupils' happiness, confidence and sense of wellbeing will inevitably be influenced by their home and school environments, and the impact of unhappiness or stress on a child's academic and social development and progress is all too well-known by teachers and parents. For this reason, pastoral care systems that are too reactive and responsive (see above) and too focused on rules and sanctions as a means of ensuring good behaviour, can fail to build self-esteem and to ensure wellbeing among pupils. More will be said later about ensuring that pastoral care is planned and monitored. Good care does not happen by accident.

The scenario of William Golding's *Lord of the Flies* reminds us that children will grow and develop in the areas listed above, whether or not any adult influence is present. As mature individuals with a greater sense of perspective and experience, it is right that we should mould the pastoral care provision to meet their needs.

Pastoral care will therefore be inextricably bound up with the school's philosophy and ethos and may be influenced by whether it is primarily a boarding or day school, whether it is single-sex or coeducational, senior or preparatory, and whether its founding mission is based on a particular religious affiliation. For this reason, pastoral care should have clear principles and objectives, and will probably be included specifically in the school's aims. In this way, all are clear about how it will be organised and delivered. It is often what makes a school distinctive.

The organisation of pastoral care

Pastoral care, as has already been said, does not happen by accident, and most schools will have thought about the primary means of achieving its stated aims.

In most schools, pupils will be assigned to a primary pastoral figure, entrusted with the care and development of the child's talents and progress. Often, this person will be a tutor or form teacher and may have a form group to look after, or be allocated pupils from different forms, possibly even from different year groups.

Occasionally, pupils are able to choose a tutor (although the motives for their choices can be somewhat varied), but more commonly the school will allocate the tutor/tutees. In boarding schools, such tutors are often house-based, and often have a dual role in providing evening cover or regular duty days in house. Other boarding schools may operate a dual system, whereby boarding house staff and tutors provide the pastoral care and support, with academic or form tutors providing the monitoring of academic progress and general development during the school day.

Whichever system is used, it needs to be effective and efficient, both in terms of use of staff time/expertise, and in producing successful outcomes for pupils. It must also be recognised that many other staff in the school will contribute to the pastoral care of pupils. Many of these will have a specialist role – such as chaplain, school counsellor and medical staff: people who will often be sought out by pupils with a wider range of concerns, because these people are perceived to be outside the disciplinary role of teachers, and are known by pupils to be sympathetic and non-judgemental listeners.

Good schools also provide alternative or parallel structures of pastoral care which will complement the formal provision in place. Staff may be allocated as mentors to individual pupils in particular year groups, or those facing difficulties needing one-to-one support. Peer mentoring or support schemes are increasingly common, and the support and encouragement of well-trained and responsible senior pupils (even in prep schools) can provide additional help for younger pupils.

Tutors should have a clear job description and understand their roles and responsibilities. It is particularly important to understand to whom they are accountable. In an extreme case (in a day/boarding school), tutors were told that they were jointly responsible to the boarding housemasters/mistresses, the heads of year, the director of studies and the deputy head (pastoral). This did not work very efficiently, particularly when it came to communication, record keeping and contact with parents.

Thought should be given as to when this tutorial and pastoral work should be done. Although the concept of relying merely on informal and unplanned contact with individual tutees may sound beneficial, it often does not work very well in a busy school. Most schools recognise that time needs to be specifically built into the school day or week to allow regular short periods of contact with tutees and the tutor group.

This is often achieved with form groups at the start of the day for registration purposes, although tutors often acknowledge that little positive or effective pastoral work occurs in this short period of time. Some schools deliver certain PSHE/citizenship topics in tutor groups in a dedicated form, tutorial or house period. Others (easier, perhaps, in a boarding school) will ensure regular contact with individual tutees at specific times of day or evening. Again, this needs to be carefully thought out and regularly reviewed. New tutors, in particular, will need guidance about the possible content of a tutor period.

Finally, tutors need to keep appropriate records which should be available to others entrusted with the care of pupils. These may involve an accumulation of academic grades and quantitative data on progress, as well as a record of achievements, key decisions made, personal circumstances and background, and so on. With sixth form pupils, links with the careers department will also be important.

It is vital that tutors are privy to necessary information held about their tutees by housemasters/mistresses and heads of year. Too often, this flow of confidential and important information downwards is less efficient than communication upwards. When allocating time for tutorial and pastoral work, it is equally important for pastoral 'line managers' to have the time to meet with their tutor teams for mutual debriefing, sharing concerns and issues, and for training.

Training to care
It should not be assumed that all staff are equally comfortable with or

enthusiastic about their pastoral or tutorial roles. Some will arrive new to the school, or to the teaching profession, with little knowledge of what it means to look after, nurture and advise young children and teenagers. Some will think they know, but might have rather idiosyncratic methods for doing so.

Effective induction for new members of staff will be crucial, as part of the whole-school perspective of overall pastoral structures, staff expectations and school pastoral and welfare policies. A comprehensive staff guidance manual will aid this process, but it will need to be explained carefully – particularly the section on the role of tutors, the child protection and anti-bullying policies and responses, and any guidance on safe working practices and relationships with pupils.

Further induction, specific perhaps to a particular year group or house, needs to be given by those specifically responsible for particular tutor teams. Having, perhaps, implied disapproval of the 'maverick' tutor employing his own particular pastoral methods, it should be acknowledged that, with experience, tutors should be able to employ some flexibility in how they respond to individual pupils and their problems.

Regular on-going training for the whole staff, and for smaller pastoral groups, will make use of termly INSET days, twilight sessions, formal meetings and informal working lunches, and will ensure that staff are updated on particular pupils' circumstances, or procedures/policies that need particular attention. The legal requirement for three-yearly training updates on the school's procedures for safeguarding pupils' welfare should complement debate about the anti-bullying strategies – things which are particularly important in an era in which cyber-bullying and other similar contemporary issues are becoming more widespread.

Training will obviously include more mundane issues such as report writing, use of available academic data and grading systems, and record keeping, but it would also be helpful, every so often, to provide training on helping pupils with emotional and social problems through conflict resolution, behaviour and anger management, counselling and listening skills, and skilled dealing with parents. New staff, especially, should be made clear about the limits and implications of confidentiality.

Improving the quality of care

The pastoral care system and framework in a school is complex and it is not always easy to know whether it is working well. It is less straightforward than the academic side of the school because of the impossibility of using quantifiable parameters and measures of success. Monitoring the number of detentions given or gold stars awarded in a term would, for example, be at best of only limited value in assessing or evaluating effectiveness.

Certainly, the views of pupils and tutors (and possibly parents) may be canvassed every so often, and this may well identify some areas that work less well than others. Some schools carry out annual surveys of pupils' experiences of their tutorial and pastoral support, with a view to modifying the structure and practices to improve the experience for pupils. Regular self-evaluation of specific areas of pastoral provision and the effectiveness of various school policies can often help to refine and improve practice. This needs to be done alongside the pastoral aims and objectives of the school.

Many schools carry out regular audits of occurrences of bullying (rates, times, places, types), the measures in place, and the effectiveness of responses. It is also worth checking the school's policy on discipline and behaviour: is its prime focus on measures to promote good behaviour and positive expectations of pupils' conduct, or does it mainly provide in great detail the different levels of sanctions to be applied to various misdemeanours? How regularly do tutors encourage pupils to set specific targets, both for academic and personal progress, and do tutors have the opportunity to discuss progress towards these targets with their tutees? Praise or small rewards for making small but significant advances can work wonders.

The pastoral 'tool box'

It is useful to have a range of skills and strategies available for pastoral work and, as in most walks of life, experience helps to develop a wider range. Among these are:

- an understanding of child and adolescent development;
- developing positive relationships;

- being non-judgemental;
- unconditional support for the child; and
- being a good listener.

Even though some staff working in preparatory schools will not have to face up to the implications of emerging adolescence in their pupils, it is instructive to remember the dogs and cats analogy at the start of the chapter. One of the trickiest situations faced by young adolescents (and their teachers) these days is the mismatch between a teenager's early physical development and their delayed emotional development (which, research suggests, still occurs in the mid- to late teens). In the early teenage years, children have much less capacity for problem-solving, rational decision-making, controlling emotions, and interpreting social cues than their physical development might suggest.

Some of the difficulties they face at school may be a consequence of normal adolescent development, masked by an unwillingness to admit they are not coping. Thus, outbursts of anger, uncooperative behaviour, failure to meet deadlines or honour commitments, and seeming lack of interest or motivation may well hide a more significant underlying anxiety.

Experienced tutors will recognise the importance of not necessarily dealing with the presenting symptoms or problem straightaway. By the same token, trying to understand and validate the underlying emotions causing a pupil to become angry will help him or her cope more effectively with the core problem.

Developing productive and supportive relationships with pupils is particularly important. One will not necessarily like every pupil whom one comes up against, but one should try to develop a relationship based on trust and mutual respect nevertheless. Tutees need to know that you are there when things go wrong and that you will be their advocate. You may disapprove of the behaviour, but not the child.

Avoid seeing things in black and white – most children are a complicated mixture of shades of grey. Although young people feel comfortable when situations and responses are consistent, recognise that you may sometimes need to be inconsistent in order to be fair, and should treat each case on its own merits. It may help, when dealing with individual tutees, to clarify what you – and they – can expect from the tutorial situation. Hopefully, most of the pastoral work of tutors will be positive and forward looking, rather than troubleshooting.

Much of this will involve asking the right questions rather than providing solutions. Hemery[4] advocates the GROW model of questioning, often used to enable those we are tutoring or coaching to focus on and identify their core needs.

Goal – What do you really want to achieve?
Reality – What is actually happening at the moment?
Options – What could you do?
Will – What will you do?

Here are some tips for new tutors to consider:

- Look for the good in all your tutees. They are all capable of great personal achievement. With your help they can be encouraged to raise their game.

- When dealing with a misdemeanour, try to identify what led up to the situation. Dealing with the root cause of problems tends to be more effective in the long run.

- When negotiating with a difficult pupil, present clear options, each with clearly understood consequences, to help the pupil make sensible choices.

- By the same token, a solution generated by a pupil will usually be more successful than one suggested by the tutor. They need to feel that they thought of it first!

- Guard against writing off a pupil. Young people can change rapidly throughout adolescence, so always be ready to forgive. They need to feel that they can make a fresh start.

- Make sure that you are clear about the school's policy for contacting parents directly, and responding to their concerns and messages.

- Give time to the 'middle of the road' pupils, as well as the very good, and those who are time-consuming.

- Always bear in mind the need to spot those who are under pressure and trying to cope with conflicting priorities, such as those who are over-stretched in many directions, and those struggling with parental over-expectation.

- Try to remain neutral when resolving a dispute between a tutee and a fellow member of staff. Misunderstanding and over-reaction can be initiated by either party.

- Recognise that the demands on pupils new to the school will usually be considerable, especially those boarding for the first time. Many new pupils will develop a protective shell to get them through the first days and weeks, and this may hide underlying concerns and anxieties. A question such as "How are you settling in?" may possibly just elicit the unhelpful response of "OK..." Don't automatically assume that new sixth-form entrants will find it easier, just because they are older.

- Don't feel that you have to know all the answers or have all the right skills. If in doubt, consult and pass concerns on, particularly when a pupil's emotional or physical wellbeing is involved.

Finally, don't expect the impossible – young people have their ups and downs and can sometimes disappoint you. Above all, enjoy your tutees' company and successes. Pastoral work is possibly the most enjoyable and rewarding job there is.

References

1. Best, R, *et al, Pastoral Care and Personal-Social Education – Entitlement and Practice*. Cassell, 1995.
2. Hamblin, D, *The Teacher and Pastoral Care*. Blackwell, 1978.
3. Maslow, A. H., 'A Theory of Human Motivation', in *Psychological Review,* 50(4) (1943): 370-96.
4. Hemery, D, *How to Help Children Find the Champion Within Themselves*. BBC Publications 0563519681, 2005.

Chapter 4

Pastoral care of very young children

Penny Oates

"I'd like to talk to you about the carrots."

Thus begins a conversation, like so many others before it and doubtless many others to come, which demonstrates the level of personalised service sometimes demanded by the parents of very young children.

"What is it about the carrots?"

"Well, my daughter/son doesn't like carrots and I would prefer her to be able to choose from a range of organic vegetables at school, just like s/he does at home."

Sometime later, after I have outlined the reasons why our catering facility cannot meet these particular requirements – although being careful to point out that we do cater for specific dietary needs and allergies (in case of later discrimination allegations) – the parent leaves feeling pleased that s/he has tested the system which s/he now understands needs to operate in this way if we are to keep the fees within bounds, honour satisfied that s/he had an extended period of 1:1 time with the Head and possibly planning his/her next challenge.

An extreme example? Definitely not, and one which is typical of the service we need to offer these days; for whilst the state of the property market inevitably swings between being a buyer or a seller's market, private education for the three to seven year-old will always remain firmly in the realms of the buyer's market. Those parents seeking to place their very young child in the care of others will be motivated to do so for a number of reasons: be they work commitments, lifestyle choice or the determination to provide their child with at least as good an education as they themselves experienced or, and preferably, an even better one.

While these reasons are both unsurprising and wholly laudable, they will be underpinned by significant pastoral expectations, since parents rightly see these as being part of the personalised service they are buying into. As parents of a two or three year-old child, which is where their journey into private education may well begin, they will ultimately be interested in academic performance, but their first concern will be how we are going to care for their child *in loco parentis*; how we will keep him/her safe and also, for some, how we will guide them through the process of being first-time parents of a school-aged child.

The pre-prep therefore takes its place on the starting line as the first leg in a relay which concludes only as the pupil moves on to tertiary education. We are the ones who establish the gold standard in pastoral matters and as the baton is passed to the subsequent members of the team (the prep and senior schools) they are charged with accepting the responsibility of maintaining the hard-won lead secured by the pre-prep staff, because challengers from competitor schools will do all they can to overtake the leaders.

In practice, this gold standard service begins with the parents' very first contact with the pre-prep school, since from this moment on, parents are either forming opinions, or seeking confirmation about what they have already heard from current parents, about the pastoral provision. They expect the Head to show them round and will have prepared many questions about details such as the school's approach to bullying and discipline, the extended day provision and why we don't take the pupils swimming. Rarely do they ask about how we teach a child to read or what our science curriculum includes.

Each family has different values and expectations, and the challenge is to remain true to the school's ethos, whilst at the same time emphasising those elements which you sense the parents are hoping to hear about. No two prospective parent tours are ever the same. All take a long time because the visitors will want to linger in the classrooms, examine the playground facilities closely and tell you about their particularly gifted child. Sometimes one parent comes as the advance party, only to be followed up by his/her partner or members of the extended family booking a repeat visit.

Once a child officially joins the roll, but before s/he begins to attend the school, there is much to be done in terms of the pastoral support of both the child and the family. First-time families welcome a home visit by our nursery staff, which provides parents with an invaluable opportunity to either ask about, or share, issues which might be worrying them, in the security of their home. If something is causing them anxiety we need to know about it because it may well have a bearing on their child's time in school, and may even go some way towards explaining unexpected or challenging behaviour. The home visit also gives the child a chance to get to know the new teachers on home territory and certainly helps him/her across the threshold on day one.

In the period before school starts, parents will inevitably receive a huge amount of information: policy documents; uniform lists; a daily routine timetable to name but a few. This can prompt enquiries for clarification, so the office staff need to be well-briefed and readily available to answer requests for detailed explanations about anything, from exactly how many items of uniform should be purchased to where parents should park at drop-off time. Experience suggests that the current parents can be a very helpful and informative resource and a booklet produced by current parents, which addresses the new parents' FAQs, will ease some of the pressure on the office.

Starting school at such a young age, and stepping up to being a full-time attendee or moving schools, can loom very large in both the child's mind and that of his/her parents. It is essential that each pupil is given individual attention and support in the first few days. This means that groups should be small, so as to assimilate each child personally. Parents never quibble about a gentle start to the school experience if it means that their child will settle more quickly. Older children joining already existing classes need just the same level of attention to their pastoral needs. Making time for them and their parents to attend a staff 'At Home' session at the school, where they can meet their new teachers on a family by family basis, provides a similar service to that of the home visit.

As time progresses and new children become part of the school community, pastoral support will naturally move away from addressing concerns about the practicalities of starting school. However, it will still focus on both the child and his or her family. Timely communication is the essence of a successful pastoral care policy. Children must understand that their genuine needs are met immediately and that staff will communicate their own view of those needs to the children's parents – in the context of how they are being seen at school, how the staff are addressing them, and what involvement the school is seeking from the parents. Since children of this age are nearly always dropped off and collected from school personally, face-to-face home-school contact is usually possible, although sometimes staff will need to ask the parent to return at the end of the day when they do not have a class waiting and can give more time to the conversation.

At this age each child needs an individualised education programme which will reflect his/her work style, level of independence and skills and knowledge base. Personal targets will be shared with and explained to parents at consultations; termly as a minimum, but possibly more frequently on a needs-driven basis – which might be either teacher or parent-initiated. Where a child is apparently failing to keep up with his/her programme, or is not meeting targets, questions will be asked as to why this is happening. This may well be because s/he has reached a plateau in learning and needs time to consolidate, or there could be pastoral reasons which need exploring. Some children are reluctant to talk about such issues, especially if they do not feel comfortable admitting to a difficulty. Sometimes the teaching assistant can be deployed to try to unravel the problem, as his/her role is generally perceived to be one of offering additional support when needed. Teaching assistants are thus an essential part of the pastoral care offered to the very young child.

The young child will generally accept that there is a need for rules and that they are expected to conform. Inevitably some will push the boundaries, for whatever reason, and it is at these times that staff need to step in to help the child to help him/herself. A clear set of school rules, which are upheld by *all* staff and regularly rehearsed in assemblies and circle times, helps to provide a framework for conversations about infringements. Rather than handing out standard punishments, which can do little more than isolate the child from his/her peers and so exacerbate the situation, it is preferable to talk about the strategies which could be used to put things right and prevent a similar situation arising again. This takes time and needs regular checks on progress. Sometimes it calls for several meetings with parents. No two children will receive the same input in such circumstances, as each reacts differently when challenged to improve and explain what went wrong in the first place.

Sometimes a young child can be unaware of asking too much of him/herself on the playground apparatus or in the gym. Whilst the obvious health and safety issues must be addressed immediately, this situation needs careful management if the child is not to feel deflated. Risk taking is part of life, but there needs to be a set of clear guidelines which allow for those with particular skills to attempt suitable challenges, whilst others succeed at their own level.

The modern child faces many challenges, some of which have always been a part of growing up. The arrival of a new sibling – or even siblings where two families combine – the fragmentation of the nuclear family and the death of a loved one or pet are just some of those life events which a very young child may have to deal with. They will have a bearing on how s/he is getting on with work, with peers and the adults immediately to hand. School must, and can, provide a safe haven. It is a place where the children are what matters to us and we must make them understand this. They must know that we will always listen and that we will not be judgemental but that if we feel it necessary we will tell their parents about their concerns. Building a trusting relationship like this with each child is possible because they spend most of their school day with the same very tight-knit group of children and the same significant adults. It is not always easy though, and it can take time. Work put in from when children join a class, which is designed to help them to feel comfortable there, will prove invaluable at times of stress.

But what of more recent trends in society? Peer pressure to possess the latest 'must-have' toy, computer game or even a particular item of clothing can cause a child considerable unhappiness. While the school cannot be held responsible for influencing parental choices of birthday treats and the like, it should not promote the desirability of such items. Sensitively discussing the child's birthday experience is much better than asking what s/he got on that special day. This can be done at a time when the child is reading with the teacher, rather than making a public exhibition of him or her in front of the whole class.

Not all children mature at the same rate and for some their awareness of the issues which used to be called the 'facts of life' is thrust upon them before they are adequately equipped to cope. Peers with older siblings or parents who believe in telling all from an early stage can unwittingly induce anxiety in their children's friends, as well as the friends' parents, when the naive child comes home with half the story or even worse, inaccurate facts. Schools can play a role here by correcting untruths and dealing with the issues in a matter-of-fact way in response to questions asked, or discussions overheard. Parents will sometimes look to the school for advice on such matters. They will find it helpful to suggest that the appropriate facts and correct biological terminology are used and that the emotional aspect is stressed.

The perception of what a school should offer parents as a whole experience has certainly expanded over the years. Nowadays time-deprived parents with very young children will seek support with parenting issues, and the Head and teaching staff are expected to be experts in this field as well as in that of teaching. These conversations generally start with comments such as, "I can't get him/her to do his/her homework/go to bed on time/eat his/her tea at the table" *etc*. This should be seen as a compliment, since it suggests that the parents respect the professional's experience and wish to replicate the school's ethos and culture in their home environment. However, it does put additional pressure on the teachers who need to come up with suggestions, often at very short notice, and who are then drawn into an ongoing review of how the child is responding.

Teachers of very young children are the ones who sometimes have to deliver difficult messages to their parents for the first time. The parent base is generally success-orientated; pre-prep parents have very high expectations of the school and their child. Teachers are there to ensure that their pupils achieve what they ought to, given their innate ability and potential. Inevitably some parents will need support when their expectations do not match the child's performance, as the parent sees it, and teachers and the Head need to ensure that the messages are given sensitively but honestly from the outset. Records of pupil achievement and supporting evidence of unaided work will help, especially when compared to that of a similarly aged pupil who is preferably of the same gender. These need to be to hand during potentially difficult meetings, because parents may prefer to lay blame on the school rather than accept that their child is not 'top of the class'.

Later on in the child's education they will come to accept the realities, but this can take several years of discussion. So, many conversations are likely to ensue and teachers will need to be secure in their findings and to be able to identify strengths, as well as the areas for development, and to offer suggestions for the parents to work on at home – often with supporting material being provided. It falls to the teacher to make sure that the child will not suffer from overload. If this seems to be the case, the parents will need to be asked to allow the child some relaxation, because the additional work is proving to be counterproductive in the classroom.

Transition to the next school can begin to feature in parents' and pupils' minds even as early as two years before it is due to take place. "Will s/he make it to...?" is a question which can dominate parent-teacher consultations if it is allowed to, even in the Reception year. While it is certainly part of our role to make sure that we recommend square pegs for square holes, such judgements are not generally wise or valid until towards the end of Year 1, in cases where transition takes place at the end of Key Stage 1. Parents need to be guided away from becoming preoccupied by issues relating to the choice of their child's next school before this stage is reached and should instead be told about their child's *current* performance and areas for development, with personalised targets being explained. When the time does come for these discussions, the teachers need to be fully briefed about the expectations and standards of the receiving school. This means that they need to spend time there.

Self-evidently the pastoral care of very young children features significantly in their early school life. Children who are starting school for the first time have no known history and we need to get to know them very quickly if we are to meet their needs from the outset. These children are, as yet, incapable of taking much responsibility for their own safety and need to be taught these skills and have them demonstrated by the adults who work alongside them. Some children need help to learn how to relate to others in their immediate space, be they peers or adults. They all need to learn about rewards and sanctions and what they represent. It is a very busy time.

Schools which cater for the very young child also appreciate that s/he comes from a family with whom a relationship based on trust and mutual respect must be forged. Parents often need regular guidance in how to optimise their child's, as well as their own, experience of school. All of this brings pressure to bear on the already very busy teacher; for consistency is the key and they cannot let up for a moment.

It falls to the senior team, and ultimately to the Head, to support the classroom staff as they provide this service for their pupils, and the parents, on a day-to-day basis. The caring and supportive culture of the school must extend to the staff who work in it. We are there to support each other and should recognise and acknowledge the strains and stresses a gold standard pastoral system brings with it. A problem shared is a problem halved.

It can at times be very challenging, but also highly rewarding. And if you are ever tempted to think that the work of the pre-prep has little to do with what goes on in schools higher up the age range, remember one phrase from earlier in this chapter: 'We are the ones who establish the gold standard...'

Chapter 5

The essentials of pastoral care in prep schools

John Baugh

He Wishes for the Cloths of Heaven
Had I the heavens' embroidered cloths,
Enwrought with golden and silver light,
The blue and the dim and the dark cloths
Of night and light and the half-light,
(William Butler Yeats)

As most of you will know, this is the first of two verses of Yeats' poem, *He Wishes for the Cloths of Heaven*, and we'll come back to the rest of it later. However, the imagery of embroidered cloths is one that I would like to stay with for now, because this is how I believe we should see pastoral care in our schools. Wherever one looks in the school, one should see the whole fabric, the whole structure, being stitched together by gold and silver threads of caring – in its widest sense – for all members of the community. This isn't something that can be bolted on or bandaged up in time for an inspection.

Our schools have always taken the care of children seriously but perhaps now more than ever it should sit at the very forefront of our thinking. "But what about the curriculum, sport, music, art and drama?" I hear some say. "None of this matters a jot if the care, safety and well-being of our children are not the most important things on our minds," is my response. First, some facts:

- Around 350,000-400,000 children live in families which are constantly 'low in warmth and high in criticism'.

- Approximately £1billion a year is spent in the UK dealing with the effects of child abuse.
- Around 36,000 children are on child protection registers.
- On average, every week, one child is killed as a direct result of child abuse and neglect.
- There are in excess of 110,000 convicted child sex offenders living in this country.
- Every perpetrator, on average, abuses 100 times before being caught.
- 25% of children experience one or more forms of physical violence.
- 11% of adults report they were sexually abused as children.
- About one-third of girls and over one-fifth of boys (aged between 12 and 15) said they were afraid, at least sometimes, to go to school because of bullying.
- 26% of recorded rape victims are children.
  (*Source - NSPCC*)

As you look out at the ranks of children at assembly or chapel, you may wonder what any of this has to do with you and your school and perhaps even what it has to do with pastoral care in *any* prep school. If that is the case, I humbly suggest two courses of action. Either you choose to read what follows and decide whether any of it is helpful to your school setting – or you move on to another chapter.

Whatever you choose to do, please at least acknowledge that this is really important stuff and, at the risk of stating the obvious, that there is never too much you can do to try to ensure the safety and wellbeing of the children in your school – or indeed the whole school community. I apologise to anyone who is offended by my approach but I believe that any complacency on our part is sheer folly.

And it isn't only about safeguarding. Happy, secure children learn better than unhappy, insecure ones. To use an awful phrase, 'It's a no-brainer'.

In order to weave our pastoral care provision into the fabric of the whole school community, we must involve *all* the adults (*all* of them) and *all* the children; everyone needs to be drawn in and it requires, to use two overused words, 'leadership' and 'ownership'.

Leadership

As with everything else, all of this needs to come from the top – the very top – and it needs to be central to the school's strategic thinking and planning. The Head and the governing body have to be very public in their desire to create a school in which the care and wellbeing of every member of the community is seen as a priority – perhaps *the* priority. This may well be done in a variety of ways:

- The Head and governors need to model the kind of behaviour they expect from everyone else. They need to 'walk the talk'. For example, being seen to bully a member of staff out of a job – even if s/he really should go – is not going to give any credibility to calls for kindness, understanding and empathy from the stage in assembly or the pulpit in chapel.

- Speeches at public occasions need to reflect the school's thinking on pastoral care and at least as much 'air time' should be given to highlighting the positive behaviour of children (and staff) as is given to academic, sporting or cultural successes.

- There needs to be a member of the senior management team responsible for managing the pastoral care throughout the school. Most schools will have this person in place but does s/he also have other major responsibilities? Does this person have a reduced timetable in recognition that this position is perhaps one of the most time-consuming in the school? Does the work primarily involve the creation and updating of policies, or is this person seen as the public face of a major department in the school? Do they chair pastoral meetings, lead training and have the same clout as the director of studies? Does this person have a proper budget to allow for the many strategic initiatives to be carried out?

- The school's strategic plan needs to have a detailed section on how pastoral care will be developed and how this development will be paid for – in time and money.

Of course this may be easier in larger schools than smaller ones, but most schools now have someone who is delegated the responsibility for curriculum development, even if this isn't at deputy head level. My assertion is that the management and development of pastoral care need to be given the same profile and that this fact needs to be publicly declared from the top.

Let us assume, therefore, that the Head and governors are taking this lead, and that someone with sufficient authority and capability has been appointed as 'head of pastoral care'. What should the job entail? The job description will vary from school to school but I suggest that it should include some or all of the following areas:

- Developing and implementing pastoral strategy.
- Working closely with others in key pastoral positions (safeguarding, counselling *etc*).
- Leading the pastoral teams and chairing relevant meetings (heads of year, tutors, matrons, health staff *etc*).
- Helping to deal with parental concerns regarding pastoral matters.
- Helping to resolve pupil relationship issues regarding bullying *etc*.
- Organising and leading pastoral training.
- Initiating research into the school's current pastoral position through questionnaires and meetings with pupils and staff (on bullying, homesickness *etc* – see below).
- Organising workshops (large and small) for parents on a wide range of pastoral issues (drugs, alcohol, sex, internet safety, parenting, bereavement, divorce/separation *etc*).
- Organising (perhaps by delegation) pupil councils – again, see below.
- Ensuring that all pastoral policies are up-to-date (linking some training around policy implementation).
- Communicating (through website, school publications *etc*) the school's policies, thinking and approach on pastoral matters.
- Providing a listening ear to children, staff and parents.

This gives just a few broad brush strokes to work with and the best advice I can give any Head is to get the right person in place, give them a proper job description (and salary) and then stand aside to let them get on with it – backing them at every turn.

Ownership

We can all be pretty stubborn at times and we rarely enjoy being told how to behave, let alone being told what to believe. My experience tells me that no amount of policies, public pronouncements or dressing downs will achieve any kind of shift in attitudes or bring about any cultural change worth talking about. This quotation from the Chinese philosopher, Lao Tzu, in the 6th century BC, puts it another way:

> True leaders are hardly known to their followers.
>
> Next after them are the leaders the people know and admire; after them, those they fear; after them, those they despise. To give no trust is to get no trust.
>
> When the work's done right, with no fuss or boasting, ordinary people say, 'Oh, we did it'.

By getting the children, staff and parents involved in setting the pastoral agenda, it is often possible to generate a real desire for change and to create some powerful momentum towards achieving one's aims. Some suggestions:

- Ask people's opinions. Survey all sections of the school community to discover how they feel about working and living at the school. Surveys are easily created using various web-based tools, for instance: www.surveymonkey.com

- People like to be asked their opinions – particularly when they can express them anonymously – and the results are always very valuable. Some areas to survey might be: bullying (children and adults), homesickness, food or use of free time, to name a few.

- Create pupil councils. By setting up appropriate councils, with elected members and properly minuted meetings (with discrete adult support), it is possible to initiate change through the children.

Children can be the most conservative people in our schools, and often most resistant to change. By giving them a voice and allowing them some say in the development of pastoral care, you should find very quickly that they are indeed proud to echo the words of our Chinese philosopher: 'Oh, we did it.' (Topics for the agenda could be: creating a pupil version of the bullying policy; use of playground space; what to do in wet weather breaks; the role of prefects.)

• Provide pastoral training each term through the expertise already available in your school. Staff are often much more receptive to the advice and thoughts of colleagues than to outside speakers. Half an hour at the start of each term is likely to be much more productive that two or three hours every two years or so.

• Engage parents in all that you are doing to develop the pastoral care in the school. Some of them will be experts in certain areas (*eg* law and health) and getting them involved will send a clear signal that you are trying to move things forward for the benefit of the whole community.

• Provide workshops for parents (see pastoral job description above) using in-house expertise, other parents or external agencies. Not only will this help parents understand and deal with some difficult issues: it will help build confidence in the school and again show parents that you are serious about the wellbeing of their children.

There are two other very important members of any pastoral team. First, the designated safeguarding officer. It isn't necessary here to go into great detail about this person's role in the school. However, a really good safeguarding officer is a godsend. When looking to appoint someone, I offer the following suggestions:

• This person should not be the Head.

• However, they should be in a sufficiently senior position in the school to command the respect of all the staff.

• They should be genuinely interested in what the job involves.

• They should be prepared to attend regular training.

- They should be willing to create links with local authority safeguarding representatives.
- They should have had experience of dealing with complex and difficult child/parent issues.

It's worth bearing in mind that one of the most stressful and complicated problems that a school could ever face may first have to be dealt with by the safeguarding officer. Having a first class person in place may be a lifesaver – literally.

Secondly, the independent listener. Each school should have someone readily available to the children who is able to offer a listening ear. This is a statutory requirement in boarding schools, but day schools too could do well to consider having a member of staff fulfil it: others choose to have retired vicars, former members of staff or local doctors.

There is nothing wrong with the latter group and I'm sure in each case they are well meaning and very good people but, if a school is serious about child welfare, why would they choose not to have in place someone who is properly qualified to listen to children? It cannot be a matter of cost because you cannot put a price on this. If the budget is tight, then re-work the budget to find a way to afford it. Evidence shows that by the time a child actually chooses to disclose at school that he or she is being abused, s/he will already have tried to tell someone seven times. Is there any price you can put on making sure that the person they speak to knows how to listen and knows what to do?

So how does all this play out in the frenetic, well-managed muddle of daily life that our schools enjoy? There are thousands of pastoral interactions taking place each day between staff, children and parents and every one of them becomes a reflection, one way or another, of the school's attitude and approach to pastoral care. Whether the school has taken the strategic decision to bring pastoral care to the very forefront of daily life, or whether things are left to evolve in the way they always have, you are sure to end up with two very different outcomes.

The following scenario is my own, but bears a passing resemblance to a short piece in Steve Biddulph's book *Raising Boys* (1997), entitled 'Hello Headmaster' (p132):

St Bolton's

It's the Thursday before half-term and Jamie (Year 6) has a history lesson just before lunch. He arrives without his books and finds it very hard to settle. After a couple of gentle warnings he is still restless and continues to disrupt the lesson. His teacher eventually loses her patience and informs Jamie that he will have to attend detention the following day, thereby delaying the start of Jamie's half-term.

Later that day, after games, Jamie wanders down a corridor and observes the Head walking towards him. Understandably nervous (the Head receives all the names of those in detention), Jamie slows down and pretends to read a notice board. The Head, who knows Jamie is down for detention, speaks to him briefly about his poor behaviour and asks him to do his shoelace up.

Jamie's behaviour does not improve throughout the day. He is noisy and disruptive in supper and refuses to cooperate at bed time. He is rude to one of the matrons and sent to see the housemaster who sanctions him with a series of 'early bed' after half-term. Jamie returns to bed and cries himself to sleep.

St Embroidered

It's the Thursday before half-term and Jamie (Year 6) has a history lesson just before lunch. He arrives without his books and finds it very hard to settle. After a couple of gentle warnings he is still restless and continues to disrupt the lesson. His teacher is aware that things are difficult for Jamie at home and he never enjoys the prospect of spending half-terms or holidays with his mother and her new boyfriend. She is also aware that Jamie's behaviour always deteriorates in the days before going home and that he needs lots of support and reassurance.

She moves Jamie to a quiet part of the classroom, says that she cannot accept any further disruptions and asks Jamie to speak with her at the end of the lesson. She manages to ignore the few remaining minor disturbances and finds a few minutes to speak to Jamie after the lesson. After a brief conversation, his teacher confirms that Jamie will be spending half-term with his mother, her boyfriend and the boyfriend's teenage son and she recognises his deep anxieties about how stressful the coming week will be.

Later that day, after games, Jamie wanders down a corridor and observes the Head walking towards him. Understandably nervous (the Head is second only to God), Jamie slows down and pretends to read a notice board. The Head, who knows about Jamie's difficulties in the history lesson, speaks to him briefly about his work, his part in the junior play and whether he is doing anything interesting at half-term. Jamie chats easily with the Head but says he's doing nothing special at half-term; his mother is working all week and the boyfriend's son "hogs the computer all the time". As they depart, the Head reminds Jamie about his shoelace.

Jamie's behaviour does not improve throughout the day. He is noisy and disruptive in supper and refuses to cooperate at bed time. He is rude to one of the matrons and sent to see the housemaster who sits him down at the kitchen table. The housemaster has already seen memos from the history teacher and the head of pastoral care and is only too aware that this is always a difficult time for Jamie.

It further emerges that the son of his mother's boyfriend is now living permanently at home and Jamie is intimidated by his loud and aggressive behaviour when the two of them are alone in the house. Jamie does not want to go home but he very much wants to see his mother. The housemaster offers to speak to Jamie's mother the next day when she picks him up for half-term. Jamie returns to bed and eventually gets to sleep.

To be continued...

Let's end it there with thanks to Steve Biddulph. I hope the point is made: two schools responding to the same problem in very different ways. At St Bolton's, there appears to be little or no system of communication. Each of Jamie's points of contact with adults happened in isolation; there was no wider awareness of Jamie's concerns about being at home or any attempt to find the reasons behind his poor behaviour. At St Embroidered, the opposite is true. Staff contact with Jamie is held together by the threads of understanding (school culture), empathy (modelling from the top), proper use of questioning (training) and communication (systems and policies). It's also clear that very sound, trusting relationships exist between Jamie's housemaster and his mother.

It's important to recognise that we cannot necessarily make the problem go away: we can only help the individuals to manage matters, and offer support to all parties. Jamie still has to go home for half term but at least he knows he is being listened to and someone understands how he is feeling. Also, Jamie's mother is now aware of his anxieties and, if she chooses to, she can now make decisions on how she can move things forward with her boyfriend, his son and Jamie. (It is also part of the school's duty of care to find out how half-term went and discover what steps Jamie's mother took to support him.)

Finally

Let us remember, as if we needed reminding, that the young lives in our care are fragile and new. Whatever our positions in our schools we all have a duty to protect and safeguard each and every child that comes our way. We have an obligation to learn all we can about how to safeguard and promote the physical and mental health of all members of the school community and, above all, we should never become complacent. A bulging cheque book and a long driveway is never a guarantee against any child becoming a sad or tragic statistic. All these young minds have their dreams and it is your duty and my duty to give them every chance of fulfilling them. As I said, this is important stuff.

I would spread the cloths under your feet:
But I, being poor, have only my dreams;
I have spread my dreams under your feet;
Tread softly because you tread on my dreams.

Chapter 6

The boarding houseparents

Dale Wilkins

Despite the rapid rate of change which has touched every aspect of our lives in the first decade of the 21st century, there can be few roles in which this change has been so evident as that of houseparents in the modern boarding school. The fact that some of our practices were virtually unchanged since the 19th century probably did not help, but the unholy trinity of inspection regimes, a huge increase in parental expectations and the blessing and curse of modern technological innovation, has made the job of the houseparent unrecognisable from that which prevailed in schools when my own career began some 20 or so years ago.

Limited facilities, poor food, strange punishments and lamentably low levels of supervision were then still all too frequent – in some schools at least – with little or no training in matters specifically related to boarding for those who were charged with the incredibly complex and difficult job of looking after other people's children 24 hours a day, and often seven days a week. 'Induction' for staff was often little more than a chat over a cup of tea (or stronger), and boarding appointments were often made with little or no thought as to the suitability of the 'applicant', who was just as likely to have been press-ganged as to be a willing volunteer.

And yet, paradoxically, the role has remained quintessentially the same. In the best houses, men and women have always given, and continue to give, willingly, selflessly and indefatigably of themselves, their time and often their emotions in order to help shape the lives of the upcoming generation. Part-time welfare officer, counsellor, security guard, banker, nutritionist, cook, call-centre operator, arbitrator, secretary, nurse, travel-agent, police officer and often removals expert, painter and decorator as well: the job has so many facets that it is hard to encapsulate them succinctly for those who have not done it, not to mention the fact that many houseparents have a different 'day job' either within the school or beyond. One is truly *in loco parentis*, only with a somewhat larger family.

Done well, and with the proper support, it is considered by many to be the most rewarding job in education today, and I count myself lucky to have learned my craft as a young resident tutor from a master practitioner who found his role, in every sense of the word, to be nothing less than a true vocation; *Every Child Matters* was, effectively, his own personal mantra, long before Lord Laming's report into the tragic death of Victoria Climbié made it every educationalist's motto.[1]

What, then, are those timeless values and qualities one needs as a boarding houseparent? Educational theorists have grappled for years with the nature of human interaction, and the way children develop in a social context. Few houseparents would argue with Vygotsky's assertion, however, that 'social relations or relations among people genetically underlie all higher functions and their relationships';[2] the contribution a good house can make to the social development of boarders is, simply, common sense.

Indeed, for many children experiencing turbulent times beyond the school gates, the houseparents and the boarding house can be the very glue which holds their fragile young lives together. Little wonder, therefore, that educational trusts and, more recently, the Department for Children, Schools and Families (DCSF) have recognised the part boarding houses have to play in helping vulnerable children. The core function of houseparenting, therefore, would seem to be to provide structure, stability and a warm, caring environment for the boarders in their care, but with sufficient flexibility to be able to drop everything in order to respond to the inevitable crises that occur.

I have always found that the course of action to be taken in managing an individual crisis was relatively obvious: if a child is missing, leave no stone unturned in looking for him or her, whilst delegating the day-to-day duties to someone else. Where houseparenting is most challenging is when crises hunt in packs, or rub uncomfortably up against the demands of day-to-day living, particularly within one's own family. It is not uncommon for both doorbells to ring simultaneously, just as the phone goes, each presenting a different difficulty to overcome, and normally when one is meant to be ferrying one's own children elsewhere, or one is in the middle of a bedtime story. Rich as the rewards are, in terms of job-satisfaction, if not financially, those contemplating houseparenting must not underestimate the impact of the job on family life, and Heads and administrators need to be fully aware of the stresses and strains too.

Regardless of whether one's spouse is employed by the school, it is almost inevitable that they will become involved in some way, if only by answering the door and fielding endless phone calls. This is often a minimum tariff, as many spouses throw themselves enthusiastically into the concept of the house as 'family'. For one's own children, living in, or alongside, a boarding community can be a remarkably enriching environment in which to grow up, with countless new friends and places to explore, but it is not without its perils. I cannot, surely, be the only houseparent to have been taken to task for spending so much time with other people's children? Schools have a duty too to acknowledge the role of spouse and children in creating the much-vaunted family atmosphere so beloved of marketing agents and prospectus writers.

Single houseparents are not immune from these stresses: they merely experience them in a different way. For any houseparents, it can often be very difficult to have any kind of life beyond the boarding house during term time. Long holidays represent a welcome, but not fully adequate, recompense. I would doubt whether there are many houseparents who adhere strictly (or even loosely!) to the Working Time Directive,[3] but it is vital that all house staff should be able to allocate themselves sufficient private time during the week, and that house and school structures should mitigate in favour of this, rather than against it.

Regardless of the size or nature of the house, whether one is responsible for one pupil or 100, one is on duty and unable fully to switch off. Yet it has also to be said that houseparents are often their own worst enemies, seemingly incapable of delegating even the simplest of tasks at times. Help and encouragement are needed here, not only by ensuring that the boarding team is sufficiently numerous to take up the slack, but also that the relevant staff are of sufficient quality. Having to leave the house under the control of someone whom one does not consider capable can be a very uncomfortable feeling and one I did not, mercifully, very often have to face. A good matron or resident tutor is worth their weight in gold several times over.

And what of those more recent challenges? There is probably still a considerable amount of water to pass under the bridge before the regulation and inspection of boarding is seen universally as a positive catalyst for change, but there can be no doubt that the spotlight pointed at the sector successively by Social Services,[4] the National Care Standards Commission (NCSC), the Commission for Social Care Inspection (CSCI) and now Ofsted, has helped to weed out many practices which were no longer acceptable. It has also given houseparents a much-needed base line from which to work, if not also a very handy stick to wield over the bursar when repairs are needed.

In some cases those schools which were not prepared to give an appropriate focus to their boarding have also fallen by the wayside: a mixture of harsh economics and increased bureaucracy has meant that only those truly committed to boarding education have generally found it viable to continue to offer it. In this regard, the sector can consider itself fortunate to have been on the front foot; uniquely within the care sector, boarding schools were at the forefront of developing the national minimum standards, through the National Boarding Standards Committee. They were also able to involve suitably trained sector professionals as part of the inspection teams, an arrangement which survived into the Ofsted era.

It is perhaps surprising, therefore, that both the standards and the ethos which underpin them remain such an impenetrable mystery to some Heads and senior managers. It is of fundamental importance that one does not become so blinkered by 'standards' (which are, after all, a minimum requirement) that one loses sight of the real aims of boarding but, as many schools contemplate their third or fourth inspection since the standards were first produced, it seems a minimum expectation, surely, that colleagues running boarding houses should receive the full support of their senior management team in ensuring not only that the standards are met, but also that everyone in the team understands their responsibilities under them, and is fully committed to a regular pattern of reflection and review.

As short-notice inspections become the norm, such a process is essential if schools are to be fully ready for a boarding inspection at any time, and it will often be the case that the frantic, hand-to-mouth existence of the modern day houseparents makes them less than ideal candidates to oversee the review process personally, although clearly they have a pivotal part to play. Indeed, where schools fall short on inspections, the problem can often be far removed from the boarding house itself, and sometimes in an area over which the boarding house staff have no control. Inevitably, however, it will be they who feel most keenly the indictment of an 'inadequate' or even 'satisfactory' verdict. Shortfalls in the areas of recruitment and child protection remain all too common (apparently contradictory guidance from Ofsted and DCSF should be no excuse), and there may still be some medical centre staff, chefs and even bursars who have little or no knowledge of the standards which relate to their areas of responsibility. Never be complacent!

Often the fault lies with a culture of misplaced trust. The concept of trust is one which is so fundamental to the way we run our schools and houses, that it is possible to be blinded by it. In such circumstances we can fail to see, or fail to look for, shortfalls which are all too readily picked up by an inspector. Heads trust management colleagues to do their jobs, and so they should, but not at the expense of accountability. The over-regulation of the state sector has, perhaps, allowed state-maintained boarding schools to steal a march in this regard, and if Heads could do only one thing to support staff in houses, surely it should be to ensure that the administrative systems and procedures are sufficient to ensure compliance with the requirements of the current regulatory framework. As the late Ted Wragg puts it in his foreword to *The School Management Handbook*: 'The best laid plans are useless if badly applied.'[5] Rather ominously, he had already intoned as his opening gambit that 'The price of mismanagement [has] never been higher'!

There is little firm evidence as to whether the advent and availability of inspection reports have made a difference to parental expectations of boarding in the way that league tables seem to have done for the academic side of education, but there seems no doubt that most modern day parents are fully versed in their roles as stakeholders. It is not so long ago that the role of the parent was to deliver the child to school; collect him or her at the next exeat and remain suitably at arm's length in the meantime. No doubt there are some parents for whom this would still be an ideal scenario (I once had a relatively local parent whom I met for the first time on the day his son left my care after four years in the house – and who then mistook me for one of the prefects), but they are becoming mercifully rare.

In her publication for BSA *Parenting the Boarder*, Libby Purves introduces the parent to the 'triangle of care',[6] and it is the task of houseparents to maintain some level of control over the flow of information around that triangle, and for Heads to support them in this.

Email and the mobile phone are a double-edged sword in this regard; the modern-day expectation of being constantly in touch is often incompatible with the demands and requirements of the wider boarding community. Admittedly, email has made the job of houseparents easier by allowing them to respond to parents as and when it suits them, yet it is not uncommon for this task to be undertaken after finally settling the house late at night. Conversely, parents can be in the habit of expecting an immediate response, even when this is impossible or impractical. Moreover, it is not unheard of for children to hack into their parents' accounts in order to give bogus permissions for visits and exeats.

Equally, the processes of reporting and accountability are often incompatible with the realities of running the house from day-to-day. Boarding staff can often find themselves torn between actually running the house, or writing up the records which prove they have been doing so! Even in these litigious times, it is essential that houses are able to have recording and reporting systems in place which support the houseparents in providing for the welfare of their charges, rather than hinder them.

The mobile phone is an equally fickle ally in this regard. Whereas the benefits of instant accessibility are often invaluable, the pitfalls are equally apparent. It is the experience of many boarding colleagues that the mobile phone has fundamentally altered the way the 'triangle' operates. All too often nowadays it is the parent demanding to know all about an incident which, as yet, has failed to come to the houseparent's attention, rather than the houseparent, in a moment of calm, after exhaustive enquiries and with justice already dispensed, ringing to advise the parent of a problem or misdemeanour now suitably resolved.

The inexorable rise in the number of younger and younger children possessing phones means that even junior houses are struggling to keep this particular wolf from the door. Young people are increasingly seeing their mobile as an extension of their very being, and it is very difficult for those of a different generation to have any understanding or tolerance of that fact. In contrast with issues such as drugs, smoking or alcohol, where schools seem to have policies from a reasonable but relatively narrow range at the more restrictive end of the spectrum, policies relating to modern technology and its policy and practice range across the entire continuum from enthusiastic acceptance to total prohibition.

It seems neither appropriate nor helpful to offer guidance on what should, or should not, be allowed; each school has to make that decision according to local circumstances. It is much easier to keep control of modern technology, I suspect, from a remote location with no network coverage and a lengthy hike to local facilities, than it is closer to the urban sprawl with its constant access and availability of the internet. What use is the most advanced screening programme if a child can circumvent the school network on a mobile phone or by buying a cheap dongle?

Far better, I would contend, for Heads to ensure that someone on the management team is fully conversant with the latest developments, and takes responsibility for briefing colleagues. This information should include ensuring that unwanted developments are understood *before* they are banned, as well as appreciating how easily students will get round them! Colleagues too need help and guidance about what is and is not acceptable. Perhaps a question for the next staff meeting would be how many staff have children's numbers in their personal mobiles, or are 'friends' with existing pupils on networking sites?

It is in respect of these types of issue that the triangle needs to be at its most potent, with a genuine dialogue between school, parent and child.

Many parents have no idea what their children are up to on-line and, despite being overtly supremely *au fait* with technology, the children themselves are often breathtakingly naive about a world which is meant to be their domain.

When taken alongside the already intense nature of houseparenting, these relatively recent developments have contributed to making the job more and more demanding year by year and, whereas acceptable ratios for supervision of students seem to nudge up inexorably in terms of their demands on manpower, the number of young staff wishing to take on boarding duties seems to be in decline. Many Heads and senior managers recognise the value of staffing boarding properly, and an increasing number acknowledge the undisputed value of training these staff specifically in matters related to boarding. When the BSA programme of professional development began in the late 1990s, the feeling was that interest would initially surge, and then plateau, but numbers on these courses continue to rise.

The value of providing suitable training opportunities for boarding staff in general and houseparents in particular cannot be understated. Heads are very adept at networking; or at information-gathering from comparable schools and in using practice and experience gathered from outside the school to review and improve practices within it. Such networking opportunities are equally valuable to houseparents too – more especially because life in term-time is lived in an impenetrable bubble. The ability to reflect on and review one's own practice, as well as to learn from others, can be a very enriching experience for both house and school, but the very nature of the job often makes it very difficult to justify the time away. Heads have an important role to play in ensuring that this vital time for review and reflection is made available, either externally via courses or within the internal structures and processes of the school.

Heads also have one other vital role to play with regard to their houseparents, and that is to help them plan their exit strategy when the time has come to relinquish the reins. Some houseparents seem able to continue for year after year with no thought of stepping down, but for others – myself included – the time eventually comes when one knows instinctively that one has no more to give to the role, and that it is time to hand on to a worthy successor. The house will have also been a home, often to the entire family, and cutting the ties may not be as simple as moving from one job to another in either emotional or practical terms. At the other end of the spectrum, there is no lonelier place to be than as a houseparent desperate to step down, but who has to carry on.

And yet, suitably managed, this time of transition can be a remarkably enriching experience, with new challenges to explore, a hand over to manage, and an appreciation that there is, indeed, life beyond the boarding house. Most of all, one can reflect on a real sense of achievement, a job well done, and the knowledge that a generation of pupils has had the very best preparation for adult life.

References

1. In 2003 the Department for Education and Skills published a green paper *Every Child Matters* in response to Lord Laming's report into the death of Victoria Climbié. In March 2009 he published an update entitled *The Protection of Children in England: A Progress Report.*
2. The eminent Russian psychologist L S Vygotsky, as quoted in Smith, P., Cowie, H., and Blades, M., (1988): *Understanding Children's Development.* Blackwell, 1998.
3. *The Working Time Regulations* (1998), amended in 2003, which set out an average working week of 48 hours, a maximum of 12 days worked in 14 and at least 11 hours rest between shifts, unless workers choose to opt out.
4. The first inspections of boarding by the care sector, as opposed to ISI, were carried out by Social Services departments in the 1990s, but only in independent schools.
5. Donnelly, J., (ed), *The School Management Handbook.* Kogan Page, 1992. Ted Wragg was Professor of Education at the University of Exeter and a regular contributor to *The Times Educational Supplement.*
6. Purves, L., *Parenting the Boarder.* BSA, 2002.

Chapter 7

Running a girls' house: what would Miss Potts have done?

Delyth Draper

At the beginning of this decade, in the wake of Harry Potter, it was called the 'Hermione Effect'. An article entitled 'Boarding School? It's magic, say girls' appeared in *The Independent* on 19th September 2002, referring to the sudden influx of girls into boarding, especially in the south-east. Enticed by the lure of 'magical adventure' and an increased flexibility that boarding schools were beginning to afford their pupils, the numbers of girls in them increased dramatically.

I often wonder what Enid Blyton, writing at the end of the 1940s, would have made of it all in a modern day revival of her *Malory Towers* series. Pondering it all over a cup of tea with a colleague recently, we joked that the risk assessments required in respect of the school's outdoor pool would have closed it down years ago, and the large dormitories would have been condemned after the Ofsted inspector had been around measuring the spaces between the beds with her metre ruler!

What is not in doubt is that the iconic housemistress in that series, Miss Potts, would have had everything sussed: her policies probably hailed as models of good practice to the other *Malory Towers* HMs, with every girl leaving her care having tremendously fond memories of her and being, in the words of the Headmistress, Miss Grayling, 'good strong women the world can lean on'.

Housemistressing enjoys many parallels with housemastering. However, leading a girls' house in the 21st century, whether it be in a single sex or coeducational school, brings unique and very different issues. Some of these remain identical to the ginger-beer-drinking days of the 1940s and others – due to the intense pressure that society now places on our young women – are complex, distinctly modern concerns, often with no single common cause.

Last year I took a prospective family around the boarding house. "What's that?" asked the wide-eyed 12 year-old. I replied dryly, "It's a payphone. You put money in it and you can call someone." There is no question that mobile phones have changed the role of *any* housemistress completely over the last decade, but especially in a girls' house. Girls can be extremely open with their parents about school issues. Some will speak once a day to their families but others seem to enjoy an almost constant conversation with home, exchanging details about every minutiae of life, remembering the smallest point or exchange that they have had with another pupil or member of staff.

The phone not only becomes a means of communication about the positive episodes, but also the negative ones. I found out once that a girl was in a detention before the teacher concerned had even entered it on the system; as a result, I was being asked by an irate mother to make a judgement on an incident that I did not even yet know had happened! Not only that, but many conversations are now had when emotions are raw and heightened, serving only to panic parents at home who then really have no other option than to call you.

Years ago, the upset individual sat in a queue for 45 minutes waiting for that now antiquated pay phone to become free; by then the incident had been forgotten and girls had to make a rapid judgement on what their precious 20p coin should be spent talking about. Practical measures, such as taking phones in from pupils at night, have to be considered, especially from the younger girls (although this must be carried out in line with the school's behaviour policy and with the full knowledge of parents). If they are not talking on their phones, they are almost certainly texting – and they will do so into the late hours of the night if they have the opportunity. There is now a sufficient amount of evidence available to suggest that mobile phone exposure an hour before sleep adversely affects an individual's ability to doze off, leading to inevitable tiredness the following day.

Whilst educating the girls themselves about the proper use of mobile phones is vitally important, so is the education of their parents. Before the beginning of a new academic year, it is worth seeing all your new parents, telling them initially to ignore any phone calls or texts that they receive during the day, so that the girls get used to seeking help from the house staff if there is a problem and thus begin to become more self-sufficient.

There are, of course, exceptions to this and, at the other extreme, there are girls who catapult themselves into the world of boarding and forget that they even have a phone. Then, two weeks into a new term you have an extremely concerned parent on the phone who is worried about the *lack* of communication. Such an issue, of course, reflects that every girl – and every parent – is different!

Experience has also taught me not to react to a situation immediately. Unless, of course, a child is in immediate danger, I no longer wade straight into an argument or into a room directly after a phone call from home (often the type of call which ends with those inimitable words from a parent: "Please don't let her know that I have called you.")

Girls need their own space and time to sort things out; they also need to gain experience in dealing both with their emotions and with those of others. A boarding school is about an education for life; we are not doing our young people any favours by magically and covertly appearing every minute the waters begin to get slightly choppy. How many times have we walked along the corridor to find said girl who was the object of the call laughing and joking with her friends, half-an-hour after the event which she has now completely forgotten about? Moreover, while she is doing this, her parents may be sitting at home, worried out of their minds – so this is the right moment for the housemistress to make that very necessary reassuring return phone call to home to put minds at rest.

When you are a housemistress, pre-empting an issue which might arise or precipitate a phone call is also crucial. If there is an on-going issue affecting many girls within a particular year, consider a group email to all parents in that year group highlighting that you are aware of it and you are dealing with it; you will be amazed by the replies you get back, thanking you for your thoughtfulness in keeping them informed. It may also bring reciprocal benefits later, in the shape of parents who can often be useful in feeding back information to you which they assume that you might already know, but in fact you did not.

Involving parents should be considered at almost every juncture as a housemistress. A parental house committee or Parents' Association can be an excellent way to involve those who are keen and willing to be involved in their daughter's education and can give more worry-prone parents a deeper insight into the running of the house and bring them on-side.

A friend of mine who was umpiring a hockey match once recalled overhearing a conversation on the side of the pitch between one irate mother, who was berating the housemistress concerned about the lack of heating in the boarding house, and another who was on the parental house committee. The committee member loyally stood by the poor housemistress, highlighting the difficulties associated with ramping up an archaic heating system and explaining the plans that were already in position to replace it next year.

What could have been an otherwise volatile conversation was dampened considerably by a parent-in-the-know. Never underestimate the power of positive parents: the combination of their contacts; life experiences; ideas and the trust they have placed in you can be a powerful combination indeed. Mums can help organise cake sales, dinners and trips out which give more experiences to the girls in your care, but without you doing the organisation – and, what's more, they love their involvement.

The nemesis of every housemistress these days centres on the issues of drugs, alcohol and sex, but they need to be addressed in specific ways with girls, and with acute sensitivity surrounding particular gender-specific concerns. With alcohol, for example, comes important discussions about how a teenage girl's appearance might seem provocative, or about how to acquire strategies to prevent an alcoholic drink from being spiked. Once again, the keys here are education and parental involvement.

Consider holding a small, parents-only forum where such issues are discussed openly, with the housemistress acting as a chairperson and facilitator. It enables those present to realise that they are not the only family struggling to find answers, or ways of dealing with a suddenly obnoxious 15 year-old girl, or the endless stream of 16th birthday party invitations which are dropping through their letterbox. More often than not, the same concerns recur every year, and simple strategies such as ringing the host of a party beforehand to check the supervision arrangements and the alcohol policy are welcomed. Parents can be used to educate one another too; don't under-rate the power of 15 other parental glares given to a mum who has just confessed to her allowing her 14 year-old to drink vodka regularly.

Teenage girls are exposed to an unenviable amount of peer pressure on such issues, and, if this does not come from friends, the media will kindly fill the gap. Magazines and newspapers are filled with stories about celebrity binge drinking and recreational drug taking and the internet now gives our young people access to *anything*. Educating our pupils about dangers thus becomes absolutely vital. It is important to follow up PSHE lessons (which may have been carried out in a coeducational class) with smaller in-house discussions for girls, once the facts have been digested and understood. It is therefore vital that all housemistresses make sure that they are aware of what issues are being taught in those lessons.

Always make the girls aware that you (or a member of your tutor team) are happy to talk to them individually about anything that is concerning them; there is such a wide maturity level within any year group in a house that some of the younger and more naive girls feel intimidated by their more confident peers: they need to know to whom they can talk.

Older pupils can also have a very positive role to play here too. Selecting carefully a couple of trained and trusted sixth-form prefects to run a session about alcohol and sensible drinking can have very effective and long lasting effects: the girls will often listen far more carefully to their contemporaries than they will to those whom they perceive to be of a different generation – especially if the advice being given is illustrated by personal experience.

Deliberate self-harm (DSH) is a distressing phenomenon which has received an increasing volume of publicity in recent years. Its inclusion in television soap storylines, and increased media coverage generally, have both raised awareness of the problem. There are a number of extremely useful courses designed for housemistresses, particularly if you do not have much experience in dealing with it. Its prevalence is difficult to determine because it is by its nature a solitary, secretive, act but a study published by Affinity Healthcare in 2008 found that one third of all girls had self-harmed between the ages of 11 to 19 years. (www.Affinityhealth.co.uk/pdf/SHS.pdf)

When approaching problems such as this, bear in mind that girls' boarding houses can often be self-perpetuating institutions; copycat behaviour can lead to enormously distressing situations arising within clusters of girls who are almost egging one another on. It is important to note that such behaviour needs addressing itself, yet can often be an external manifestation of other problems. Each individual needs to be listened to; guided; offered other avenues of help if necessary; and she should never merely be dismissed as attention-seeking. Whatever form the DSH may take, it is crucial that when you discover it, whether it be from another pupil (girls are excellent at telling you when they are concerned about their friends) or through the pupil telling you herself, you do not react as if you are shocked.

Stay very calm. Be quite pragmatic if necessary and practical, rather than judgemental and disapproving. Every school will have its own policies and structure to give you support, help and advice, so it is vitally important that you are familiar with updates and where to find the avenues of help quickly. Always consider the others in the year group too; they will need help and advice in how to support their friend and you need to make it really clear that communication between them and you is vital.

They will like the fact that you are trusting them and giving them a responsible role, but this trust must also be cushioned with a very strong network of support and help. I am increasingly being asked by parents about DSH: what do I do about it and does it exist in my house? I am always honest; houses are microcosms of society and I would be foolishly deluding the individual who had asked the question if I was to deny any knowledge of it ever existing. I do, however, explain clearly how I deal with such issues; how the girls support one another and how crucial a supportive and open home is in preventing such matters arising in the first place.

Anyone who has ever had even the slightest contact with girls will know the falseness of that age-old saying: 'Sticks and stones may break my bones, but words will never hurt me.' Boys may be able to sort out their disagreements with a quick punch-up, but girls use much more devious and undetectable tactics and 'bitching' is a prime weapon in their arsenal. Girls bitch because group judgements provide them with crucial guidance as to how to look and behave, when they feel most vulnerable about who they are. They bitch to turn attention away from their own weaknesses and it seems so easily to become part of their everyday dialogue with one another.

Negative body language can be equally cunning – a sly glance, a blank or refusal to sit somewhere – and such subtleties can easily go undetected in the classroom, sinking below the radar of a busy housemistress. Bitching in a boarding house can be the most destructive of all behaviours. It unsettles year groups, leads to a prickly feeling which diffuses throughout the entire house and it often causes irreparable damage. It is imperative that those who suffer at the hands of such conduct need to have their situation acknowledged by an adult. It should never be ignored or considered as simply 'girls being girls'.

The ethos that a housemistress creates, and the resultant atmosphere, is therefore of paramount importance. Older pupils have a vital role to play in stepping in and making it clear that such comments are not welcomed in their community. When you train your house prefects, you should stress this point, stating how important their behaviour is in modelling positive relationships. I always mention it at the beginning of year house staff meeting too. It can be tempting for a young or inexperienced tutor to probe a pupil for some gossip about a staff colleague, but tutors, matrons and domestic staff must mirror the relationships that you want the girls in the house to have with one another. Respect is so crucial at all levels. Girls need to respect one another's strengths and weaknesses and to know that derogatory or disparaging comments about someone else's shortcomings will simply not be tolerated.

Celebrating success (both individual and collective) across the board is so important, too. Use house assemblies to recognise all levels of achievement and across each activity, so that every house member is aware of the talents and strengths of all in their community. However, girls need to know how to work towards their goals but not at the expense of their physical, mental and emotional wellbeing. Boarding schools could be criticised for churning out the oppressive paradigm of the 'perfect girl'; nowhere is this more apparent than when looking at their approach to academic work.

Girls tend to be self-motivators and can often be fiercely competitive with one another. They will look only at the effort grade given, rather than the comment going alongside it – and then they will compare their mark with everyone else's. If a girl is told to spend 30 minutes on a piece of prep, she will spend an hour on it and those with perfectionist tendencies will rewrite a piece of work several times until it is considered utterly flawless.

It is therefore important for the housemistress to maintain balance within an individual's programme, enabling her to keep a much greater perspective on life. This will also put the pupil on the road to living a healthy and productive life, rather than one which is fuelled by an unhealthy drive for perfection, which eventually leads to her crumbling under the weight of her own expectations.

Staff often need educating about this. If you have an individual who consistently (and unreasonably) goes beyond the parameters of an assignment, speak to the teacher concerned and ask him or her to set clear boundaries – for example, a word limit which, if exceeded, will result in a poor mark. Consider running small workshops with groups of girls on note taking, with the emphasis on being how to work *smarter* rather than harder; they essentially need to know when 'good enough' is, indeed, good enough.

Girls can be acutely sensitive within the classroom too and an ill-judged sarcastic remark can leave them feeling humiliated and worthless. Girls are more likely to internalise such negative perceptions which will, in turn, lead to low self esteem. Such colleagues are, thankfully, rare in today's classroom but a quiet word from you will not go amiss, ideally pre-emptively rather than reactively. It is also important to speak to sensitive pupils and equip them with the skills that they need to deal with situations when they arise, concentrating on quietly assertive sentences that they should remember and use.

A pivotal factor in the running of a girls' house – and the one which not only permeates this issue, but every matter in this chapter – is that of self-esteem. Girls' self-esteem peaks at about nine years-old and then tends to plummet. The internal and external pressures that today's girls face – body shape; boys and sex; society's demands on them to conform rather than celebrate their individuality – mean that their appearance becomes an all-consuming obsession and, in some, the only measurement of self-worth.

In our media-frenzied society, one might argue that a housemistress can have little impact on the development of a healthy self-esteem within her boarding community, given the other factors that she is competing against. However, by interweaving several core messages into the day-to-day running of the house, much good work can be done to help change patterns of thinking. New ways of facing life's challenges can then be created, building an emotional resilience which will stand the girls in excellent stead not only throughout their school career but beyond.

Remembering to praise individuals for their successes is easy but housemistresses need to address perceived failure too. Making a pupil feel good about being selected for the B squad is just as important as congratulating those who have made the A team. Always try and turn a supposed failure into a success for an individual, getting her to see the positive side of a particular situation.

In this context, I always advocate having 'a man in the house': in other words, there should always be a male member of staff within a tutor team! Men tend to be less protective and they break down stereotypes, helping to keep perspective, a sense of balance and 'real-life'. They, alongside and in a complementary way to you, can encourage the girls in your house to try new things.

If your school does not have an already well-monitored extracurricular programme, set one up in-house, to ensure that every girl is gaining a broad experience. The more things individuals try, the more likely they are to find a niche; something they are good at; something for which they can be praised.

Physical activity is an important factor in this. Those who engage regularly in such activity have enhanced mental health; reduced symptoms of, or propensity to, depression; and an outlet for their stress. This is not normaly an issue with junior pupils who usually have several hours of compulsory games time each week, but it is vitally important amongst older girls.

Those who have outgrown the traditional team games should be given alternative options: yoga, pilates and fitness classes for example. Successful games programmes for sixth-form girls really encourage those participating to be fit for life; they also promote healthy attitudes amongst often disaffected games players.

Above all, it is important to consider your own comments and behaviour, and how they might be perceived by the young women in your care. It is important for them to realise that you have made mistakes and are not infallible, but that you have come through them a stronger and more confident person.

The role that the family plays, too, within the development of self-esteem is central to everything that the school is trying to do. Some families are excellent; others need some prompting in the right direction, and it is the role of the housemistress to do this if necessary. An email or phone call stressing just how much improvement a girl has made, or highlighting in your newsletter the high standard of netball played by the 4th VII team at the weekend, are both vital in bringing parents into harmony with your ethos.

Never be afraid to advise a parent to give their daughter a pat on the back for something, however trivial. A very significant yet fundamental factor in developing and unlocking potential in girls (it is also a vital ingredient in the development of trust in girls too) is, quite simply, to believe in them. Those four words, 'I believe in you', are incredibly potent; they enable an individual to realise that there is someone who genuinely cares about them. This is often the first step for that person starting to believe in themselves. For some girls the ability to achieve a healthy level of self-esteem remains elusive throughout their school career, but I have a firm belief that even these individuals will carry some of the messages away to university or jobs with them, and will eventually grow into stronger and more confident women.

Cruelly, there does occasionally come a time when the needs of one individual must be weighed up against the entire house: for example, if there is someone who is seriously out of place in the house and failing to thrive in it, or continually poisoning the atmosphere and eroding its ethos. At such times, some difficult and sometimes life-changing conversations must be held with the girl concerned and her parents.

Such conversations should not come out of the blue, however, and should be the culmination of many months of dialogue with both the parents and pupil – unless, of course, the situation makes it quite impossible to act in this way. Colleagues on the senior management team can be exceptionally supportive and it is imperative that you do not carry the whole pastoral burden in such situations. Being able to share such issues and talk about them are both strengths in a good housemistress: we advocate the pupils talking openly and it is important that we also practise it ourselves.

Someone unconnected with girls' boarding might read a chapter such as this and make the comment that they wouldn't touch the job. That melting pot of hormones in the midst of what can often be a highly competitive and pressurised environment is not for everyone, but it is easy to forget how compelling, engaging and rewarding working with teenage girls can be.

To witness them arriving at the age of 11 or 13 and seeing them through the exhilarations and despairs of puberty; guiding, helping and ultimately watching them grow into well-balanced young women fills all who carry out the role with a deep humility. It can be easy to lose sight of this tremendous privilege that all housemistresses have, especially with the increased – and increasing – burden of paperwork that all face, but the rewards of such a position cannot be measured, as they are in a classroom.

Moments of deep joy when you share a success or help someone to achieve an ambition are utterly priceless and girls can be tremendously appreciative of your efforts. Girls are also much more likely to stay in touch and keep you updated with their news too; to know that you have played a small part in helping someone on that journey of self-discovery, growth and possibly the achievement of a dream is a very special thing.

We all have much to learn from the young people within our care – their tremendous enthusiasm and zest for life, their focus and unbridled ambition. Boarding schools are terrific places for our young women to thrive and flourish, but it is ultimately the role of the housemistress to ensure that the environment in which they are carrying out that crucially important task is happy, supportive and well balanced.

Girls can be like pressure cookers and perhaps the measure of a good housemistress in the 21st century is being able to know how to open that valve now and again to disperse some of that steam.

So what would Miss Potts make of it all? Would Darrell Rivers, the schoolgirl heroine of the Enid Blyton *Malory Towers* books, be whisked away at the end of her first half-term for anger management counselling? What would be made of poor old Gwendoline Mary Lacy's obsession with the rich and glamorous? Filling in her on-line Ofsted self-assessment form, I think she would probably observe that girls really had not changed very much at all.

Chapter 8

Boys' housemaster, then Headmaster

Christopher Hirst

Harold Wilson, no great friend of independent schools, once testified to the speed of change in government affairs with the observation: "A week is a long time in politics." In the year in which I entered teaching, he was Leader of the Opposition, between his two terms as Prime Minister. Looking back from the vantage point of nearly four decades as teacher, housemaster and Head, it seems apparent that the same is true of education; we have been through a period of prolonged and relentless change. This includes the National Curriculum; regular, universal inspection of independent schools both by ISI and social services agencies, and many of the other developments already charted in chapter 1 of this book. The combined effect of them all has been to put housemasters (and Heads) at risk of being overwhelmed with administrative paperwork, diverting them from the true nature of the role.

During this period, boarding schools have reinvented themselves in all sorts of ways. Some have gone for radical innovations such as flexi-boarding and fixed weekend exeats for all. Some have downsized; others have become coeducational. A few – mine included – have opted to preserve boarding in its most distinctive form, with individual boarding houses responsible for catering and feeding.

Most schools have become much more accessible to parents, by welcoming them more positively to a wide variety of school events and laying on an increasing number of parent consultations. Even though the principle of having no weekend exeats during the first three weeks of a pupil's first term at their new school often remains, it now seems extraordinary that only a generation ago many schools advised parents to stay almost entirely out of even telephone contact with their children during that period. Contact on demand between home and pupil has been revolutionised by the mobile phone, the internet and email – bringing great benefits but also some interesting challenges for schools.

However, for those most deeply involved in pastoral work in a boarding school, a great deal has *not* changed. The best practitioners are still totally immersed in it in a unique way. The workload and qualities that it presupposes, and the stamina it requires, are enduring. The excitements of helping members of your house to discover or acquire new talents are just as important as ever they were. The privileges of helping to shape young lives are just as real. The technologies of the workplace may change radically, but so much of school work still centres around human nature and the demands of helping *people*.

So what advice might it be useful to pass on to those embarking on housemastering, this most demanding yet most rewarding of roles? To avoid complications of terminology and as this chapter is primarily about the pastoral care of boys, I have mostly expressed ideas in terms of the male gender.

Whatever else you do, *know your boys*. Why? Because from this, almost everything else follows. In good times, it enables the house to become far more than the sum of its parts; in difficult ones, a parent will forgive (you) almost anything if he or she perceives that you are essentially close to their son; that you empathise with him even if you have to be tough with him; that you haven't forgotten what it is like to experience the teenage years and the mistakes and errors of judgement that can come with stretching wings and testing limits. When there is bad news to pass on, have the confidence to pick up the phone to give it, rather than hiding behind written communication.

Remember to create an ethos and spirit in your house that means you will enjoy being a part of it. At times this will involve instilling a sense of discipline and order which gives it structure and firm boundaries – which is what boys essentially like, and respond to. While they don't instinctively warm to appeals to logic and statements about the importance of systems, they don't defy experience.

Let your house reflect the best side of your character, not the worst. If in doubt, err on the side of strictness – especially in the early stages. You need to win respect and you must show that you have clout and that you have established control. Never compromise on issues of safety, bullying and child protection, and never turn a blind eye to disciplinary issues if there is the slightest chance that your boys, knowing you have done so, will think you have done it in order to take the line of least resistance. But respect also has to be earned – so when you can, show your sense of humour, and your sense of proportion; your kindness and sensitivity to the views and feelings of others. Set an example to your pupils in the courteous way in which you treat your house staff.

Be highly visible around the house. On balance, err on the side of total involvement and immersion: you must know what's going on. Cultivate your antennae and develop an intuitive sixth sense when it may be time to act. But try too to work through your prefects, rather than leading and supervising everything. They need the opportunity to manage the house within the limits that you set; there are some issues on which they will carry more influence with younger boys than you will, simply by virtue of being closer to them in age. At times there can be advantages for you in a slightly more detached style of paternalism.

Try to recruit house tutors who are complementary to you in interests, skills and outlooks, rather than look-alikes. Every boy needs to find at least someone in the house 'team' with whom he empathises, so if you are a gung-ho games player, you need others whose interests lie more in (say) the arts. Go the extra mile with boys in showing an enthusiasm for things which matter to them but which do not particularly excite you – or which you know little about. You may surprise yourself... One of the biggest identifiers of a really top-class house is how well it contains, steers and channels the energies of its more imaginative, questioning and divergent pupils.

Keep your tutors fully informed, and remember to appreciate what they do. Use them to the full in monitoring boys' work. Whilst many boys thrive on the demands of A level, there is a growing body of evidence about the extent to which they are generally far less academically motivated and well-organised than girls in the years to GCSE – so they need the best safety-nets that we can devise. And, while your boys are indeed 'your boys', no housemaster these days (however outstanding), can be an expert on everything. So use to the full those in your school who specialise in A level choices, university entrance *etc*. Encourage the best possible liaison between house matrons (if your school has them) and the nurses in the school medical centre.

When you hit an intractable pastoral problem, don't be afraid to share it with a fellow-housemaster. In many schools the competitiveness between houses (and housemasters) can be very creative, but taken to excess it can also be stifling and unproductive. While good games players often make good housemasters because of their identification with, and experience of, teamwork and self-discipline, they are not always the first to see that there is sometimes more to life than competition! Here too, keep things in perspective... However, boys are mostly competitive – and you can harness this instinct not just through games, but also in organisational ways such as charity fundraising.

Forge constructive relationships with your non-housemaster colleagues. When they offer to deal with a problematic member of your house, capitalise on their willingness and exploit their skills, recognising that sometimes they will be able, better than you, to unlock a tricky pastoral issue. Back them up when they need it. Conversely, don't let them dump classroom disciplinary issues on you which they should be sorting out themselves, and don't allow them to vent their frustrations on you unreasonably for things which your boys have (or have not) done. Do all you can to keep your teaching lively and up-to-date, and your marking done to time. Housemasters have so many calls on their time, but many of them began their careers as outstanding teachers; too many then tend to find themselves withdrawn too much from the classroom. Your teaching can also be a welcome form of variety (even a release) from the demands of housemastering.

Try to be a forceful marketeer for your house and your school. This is a new demand on you since the days when I first became a housemaster. A full house is a happy one, because people feel that belonging to it is a privilege. Play your part to the full with prospective parents; some of the most rewarding (and later, grateful) ones are those who are coming into contact with boarding schools for the first time. Set out to show them that we are not posh, and be aware of how much our schools benefit from social mix and diversity.

Remember that housemastering is a long-distance race. Don't try to make too many changes all at once in the early stages (unless you have taken on a house which needs completely turning upside down), and resist the temptation to take on too many other things. On the other hand, try to have at least some outside interest, and to do periodic INSET. Take opportunities to go to area gatherings of housemasters from other schools: it helps you to realise that the grass isn't always greener elsewhere, and that a problem shared is a problem solved.

As much as you can, give your family the time and space that they need. Make the most of your holidays, and get away from the school.

Remember that something good will happen every day; that you are touching someone's life every day, and that they will remember you for it. Don't be overwhelmed by difficulty and look for the best things in any given day. The inspirational housemaster is a great actor: if *you* don't appear cheerful and on top of things, people will imitate you; if you do, they will respond to you.

Go browsing in second-hand bookshops for a copy of Ian Hay's *The Lighter Side of School Life* (or buy a reprint from John Catt Educational Ltd, the company which publishes this book). Written in 1914, its chapter on 'The Housemaster' contains much that you will recognise, even a century on from when he wrote it. You may also agree with his statement:

> A bad headmaster cannot always prevent a school from being good. But a house stands or falls entirely by its housemaster. If he is a good housemaster, it is a good house; if not, nothing can save it. And therefore the responsibility of a housemaster far exceeds that of a Head.

And then eventually, as I did, perhaps you will choose to become a Head yourself.

In many ways, as a Head, you have moved into a very different mode of life. You have direct responsibilities to many more constituencies –

including governors, staff, former pupils, friends and potential donors; the public at large. You are in the front line in marketing your school to individual parents and to feeder schools. You face familiar challenges on a much larger scale – for example, effective communication. There may be new ones relating to financial management and efficient administrative structures which will ease the burden on the teaching staff as a whole and on housemasters in particular. To an extent that few appreciate, you are directly answerable to your employers, the governors. The buck truly stops with you.

You experience in a new way the dilemmas of what to delegate, and what not to. You feel taken for granted when things are going well, yet suddenly in great demand when something goes wrong. You have to learn to become even more accepting of periodic crises – and of the fact that others sometimes make mistakes whose consequences you then have to mop up. You have to write many more little notes of appreciation – especially to someone whom you have forgotten to mention in your speech or vote of thanks. In this respect (and in many others) you learn to put your mistakes behind you and to move on rapidly.

Much of what follows revolves around relationships between Head and housemaster. There is a good reason for this. You also have to learn to become less of a direct initiator and more of an enabler at one remove: working pastorally and making things happen through your housemasters. Yet even after 25 years as a Head, I tend to feel that once a housemaster, you are always a housemaster. You never stop being one, unless your school is exceptionally large. In one sense you feel yourself as housemaster of a larger house with your housemasters in a similar relationship with you to the one that you formerly enjoyed with your prefects – although there are very significant differences, too. You use the same antennae to discover what is *really* going on; the importance of good communication remains, but grows; you continue to use the skills and empathy that you developed as a housemaster.

Maybe I feel this particularly keenly because I represent something of an increasingly rare breed – the housemaster-to-Headmaster-in-one-jump, with no post as deputy head in between. However, even though I never held such a role, I'm convinced that it is (whether you call it 'deputy head', 'sub warden' or whatever) an increasingly important one in ensuring good relationships between a Head and his housemasters. It's a partnership which you have consciously to cultivate; especially when you are new to the school, and your deputy has such an important role to play in helping you to understand what makes your new school tick, combining the role of being your adviser simultaneously with that of 'keeper of the school ethos'.

In a decentralised, non-campus school such as mine the importance of getting out and about to lunch and to evening visits to houses cannot be overstated. The weekly meetings with housemasters individually and collectively, are vital too; the housemaster body has to be bonded into one based on shared experience and close mutual loyalty. The boarding school thrives on that delicate balance between houses of unique identity and individuality without too much fragmentation and uncertainty or inconsistency of approach between them.

As a Head, you both rely on your housemasters *and* appreciate them for all the heat of the day that they spare you. It goes without saying that they need your full support in public, even if occasionally you need to remonstrate with them in private. They also need the security of knowing that you won't duck the difficult issue of suspension, required removal or expulsion when a situation demands it – even in those difficult times when the needs of the house as a whole have to come before those of an errant individual with extenuating circumstances.

They may, however, also need educating about the legal and other demands on you in an age of rights of appeal against expulsion: no-one understands the pressures and loneliness of this sort of decision until, as a Head, they have been called upon to make it, and we have all sat around in common rooms in our time saying to each other: "I just can't understand why the Head has ducked this one..."

It is a vital part of your job to pass on your experience; to help housemasters grow into, and in, the role; and to nurture their potential successors, aiming wherever possible to give them residential experience initially as house tutors. You need to aim to have a housemaster body which is varied in personal style, temperament, outlook and interests so that you can match the maximum number of parents to someone with whom they will develop a good relationship. If your school is periodically short of potential housemasters, it is better to advertise outside than to be tempted to appoint people from within at too early an age. In some ways it may seem a younger person's job these days, but you do neither them nor their charges any favours if you give in to the temptation to give them the job before they are ready for it.

Don't always expect your housemasters to behave or react exactly as you did in similar circumstances. Resist the temptation to drive them too hard: the fact that you became a Head suggests that you are exceptionally driven. By contrast, your housemasters may not be – and they may be even better housemasters than you were precisely because of that fact. Be aware too that one of the most frustrating sides to preparing to leave a school is the knowledge that you will not be there to see the success of those whom you have prepared for the role.

In a school with strong constituent houses, there will be times when you need to be a skilled referee, balancing carefully your support for a housemaster with that which you give the bursar. You need to avoid undue expenditure or extravagance; to promote fairness between houses, and to ensure that he who shouts loudest is not necessarily he who gets most. On the other hand, enterprise should be rewarded: for example, in the case of a housemaster who has lived regularly and uncomplainingly through the demands of extensive holiday lettings.

There may be times when you will have to make a difficult decision in respect of a housemaster who is also a five-star teacher (the two things often go together). The bursar will want teachers deployed to the full because it is his job to do so; the director of studies may well have been told that it is his job to produce an economical timetable, and the head of department may well say that he can't do without one of his best performers. However, the housemaster concerned may be asking you to avoid him becoming completely overloaded – or he may even need to be protected from himself and from his own inability to say "no" in taking on even more of a role he loves. Again, you will be the referee.

You also have a responsibility to see that your housemasters don't go on so long that they are too battle weary for either their own good or that of their boys. When they leave their houses they may well have another ten or even 15 years to give to the school, and it is part of your job as Head to see that their long and varied pastoral experience is not lost to it.

This may be, for example by playing a major role in the ever-increasing importance of thorough NQT induction, but it can also continue to be used within the house system. At one time former housemasters were sometimes prised out of pastoral work altogether and steered reluctantly into roles for which they were not always suited (such as running the careers department), or worse still left without any meaningful role.

More recently, however, there has been a very positive development towards encouraging them to join a tutor team in another house. This enables many to capitalise not only on their own housemastering experience of boys, but also that of having been a parent of teenagers themselves. In the process they can also act as mentor to a new housemaster whose own children may be much younger. Is it too fanciful, I wonder, to envisage a future which includes a cadre of experienced former housemasters, available to share their experience with other schools which may for a time have particular need of it?

It is sometimes said that 'historians imagine the past and remember the future'. I hope I have avoided the former, but what will the shape of boarding education be in another century's time? Possibly fewer schools, dealing with larger numbers, in order to achieve continuing high quality provision through financial economies of scale. Yet the role of the housemasters will continue to be crucial, and the pastoral commitment and skills that they bring to bear on a school will do much to define both its substance and its reputation. I hope too that even though so many of the details of day-to-day life may have changed, there will still be much truth in the essence of another passage from Ian Hay, even if in 1914 he wrote it partly tongue-in-cheek:

> The life of a housemaster is a living example of the lengths to which the British passion for taking heavy responsibilities and thankless tasks can be carried. Daily, hourly he finds himself in contact (and occasionally collision) with boys for whose physical and moral welfare he is responsible... But he loves it all. He maintains, and

ultimately comes to believe, that his House is the only House in the School in which both justice and liberty prevail, and his boys the only boys in the world who know the meaning of hard work, good food and *esprit de corps*.

Chapter 9

Pastoral care of staff

Richard Harman

Shortly after I had been appointed to my first Headship I went on holiday to America. On the beach in North Carolina I met a woman who was well into the latter stages of her career as a Head. She asked about my career and I told her of my recent appointment. She looked at me steadily for a few seconds and then simply said: "Ah, yes, a lot of listening."

Although the joys and challenges of Headship are many, and the decisions made every day are legion, what is perhaps most surprising is how much one is called upon to listen, to attend carefully to other peoples' stories, to be really present for each individual even (especially) in the midst of pressing crises. And, as Head, the pastoral care of staff takes on a much greater significance than it did previously. The teaching staff take on the front-line work of caring for the pupils, but who cares for the carers? And on a more basic level, which individual in an organisation doesn't want to be recognised and acknowledged by the boss?

I run a large boarding school in a small market town in Middle England. Yesterday my wife went to post some letters at the post office in the market square 200 yards from our house. The short errand took her well over an hour. The conversations she had on the way to, in, and on the way back from, the post office encompassed colleagues from both the teaching and support staff. They covered all kinds of topics in their daily lives, including births, marriages (and marriage troubles), and bereavement.

Arguably this work is just as important to a school community as the work I do at my desk and probably it is much more important than 50% of the email correspondence I have to deal with. The Head's spouse can play a significant role in making the staff feel cared for. Schools vary in type and context; unmarried Heads will have different strategies and all

Heads and their spouses will vary in their approach – but if circumstances and attitudes allow, there is a deep pool of need for the 'first couple' in most schools to be seen as parent figures for the whole community.

Why is the pastoral care of staff so important? Put simply, our staff are our biggest and most important resource (something we are fond of repeating, but about which we probably do too little) and they need to be looked after in all sorts of ways. They are our most expensive asset (salaries are by far the biggest cost in our schools) and the quality of the people employed, teaching and support staff, defines a school. Their work is exhausting, and during an increasingly busy and pressurised school year it can take a toll on both them and their families.

If they feel well supported and cared for, we are likely to have happier and more productive schools – and the pupils, the focus of all our work, are likely to have a better experience of school as a result. Not only that, but the culture of the school as a whole will be stronger, which in turn will attract more parents and pupils to it. I speak from a boarding school perspective, unashamedly, but I strongly believe the same principle applies to day schools, even if there is less time and opportunity in the school day to attend to the pastoral needs of each individual.

'Busyness' is a feature of all our schools and at pressurised times of term it can overwhelm the best of intentions, but I do strongly recommend the 'power of five minutes' and the importance of 'management by walkabout'. Being seen around the school; setting an example of being present in various different places (varying the routine and route); spending just a few minutes at a time attending to the concerns, small or large, of colleagues from a cross-section of school life, are absolutely invaluable. Aside from anything else, you will learn an enormous amount, and you will also gather information that you could not get any other way but with your own eyes, ears and instincts: you are there in person.

Management by walkabout (MBWA) can in turn contribute strongly to what I call 'pre-emptive leadership'. This seeks to deal with issues and anticipate challenges before they really get going. It keeps the momentum with you and is a much more powerful tool for change management than any number of meetings or any amount of reading of documents, important as these are in the mix.

It helps with efficient administration because you have a better idea of what is important and what can wait or be delegated; it helps with good management by gathering information; it helps you to have a personal interest in, and knowledge about, what is going on; and it is a central aspect of good leadership by setting the example and being seen.

It is a truism in the military that soldiers like – and need – to see their generals at the front line. It keeps morale high and alerts you to areas of resistance or cynicism. And this is all part and parcel of the pastoral care of staff: there is no real gap between doing pastoral care of staff well and being good at leadership, management and administration.

Formal processes are vital too: I imagine that virtually all our schools now have well-developed appraisal and CPD programmes and these are very important and helpful systems. There needs to be a formal and timetabled space for reflecting on practice and seeking to improve it – and this too is about bringing the best out of, and developing, our staff in all sorts of ways. But the formal and informal should ideally fit together seamlessly. Pastoral care and professional development of staff should be integral parts of a whole-school approach to looking after the people in our organisations. It is about school culture.

The best organisations increasingly have a culture where this is being done all the time. An ongoing, holistic conversation takes place, encompassing managers and managed in a free flow of information, ideas, support and suggestion. Individual people are seen not just as functional members of a greater team, but also as whole beings with their own pastoral needs: this is where we should be aiming even if, as very hierarchical places, schools are pretty far off the ideal at present. We need to be on that journey and consciously working to improve our school culture. Ideally, the pastoral care of staff will overlap and merge with our systems of professional development, so that the formal conversation becomes an extension, development and crystallisation of innumerable informal ones.

Meanwhile, even in our less-than-perfect hierarchies, people want and need to feel recognised and known by the person at the top of the pyramid.

Taking a passing (or more properly a real, if necessarily time-limited) interest in a colleague's family is of great value to them. I still remember how one former Head of mine knew the name of everyone's child and pet and would ask after them regularly and with real warmth. This established the nuclear family of each colleague as being embedded in the extended family or community of the school as a whole. Not all of us can instinctively do this aspect of leadership as well or as energetically as this Head (who was a past master at it), but it goes with the territory of headship, perhaps tapping in to that part of the role which is about being a tribal chieftain; it is a skill we all consciously need to develop in our tool-kit.

There are techniques that can help those to whom it comes less naturally, and whilst some of them may seem mechanical, they do work. I recommend at least an annual update of a school-wide staff 'Who's Who' document (either on paper or electronic), with photos and other relevant (and data protection compliant) information. This can be useful for recognising newcomers and learning the names of family members, which is particularly helpful when you are new in post.

Ideally it is a resource that should be available to all new colleagues, though no doubt various permissions will need to be sought. Providing hospitality for new and established staff together in a well-planned but not too daunting way helps to build community and to set up cross-departmental networks of social support. In the press of a hectic term it can be surprising how grateful people are to be coaxed out of their silos for a while if the atmosphere is convivial and fairly informal.

In terms of taking care of staff there are particular demands on the Head of a smaller school. Here you will be expected to know everything and everyone, and to do much more of the legwork yourself because the staff themselves have to wear many hats at once. In this case it is very important to keep a close eye on the school calendar, to ensure that events are not out of control in any given week.

In a bigger school the key will be to find the right people to delegate these tasks to, so that even though you cannot keep a close eye personally you know there is a trusted and competent person who is doing so. Members of the SMT, HoDs, houseparents and heads of pastoral section all have a role to play in seeing that members of their respective team are fully integrated into the school as newcomers, and in watching that they do not become too over-worked or over-stressed once established.

Having said that, rather than seeking the ideal work-life balance in term-time (which is a minefield in our schools, made even more hazardous by the advent of the Working Time Directive, parental leave and employment regulation *etc*), perhaps we should be helping staff to find the right work-life integration. An ability to manage the demands of both school and home seamlessly and simultaneously, with the right support in doing so, rather than trying to separate them out, may be a clue to the way forward. This is of course easier said than done and as a starting point it is vital to remember that all individuals are different. What is a source of energy and excitement for one colleague may be a source of stress and misery for another.

Meanwhile the person at the top needs also to exercise an overview: as Heads we all need to watch out for a tendency to celebrate the busyness of our school (very important and marketable!) at the expense of balance in everyone's work and lives and a particularly frenetic edge to the school's culture. Are we good enough at deciding that certain activities have passed their sell-by date and need to be wound up?

Some colleagues will need protecting from themselves. Be alert for those who take on more and more, becoming increasingly highly energised until at some point they explode. There is much truth in the correlation which lies behind the saying, 'If you want a job done, give it to a busy person,' but we have a duty of care to look out for these signs of self-inflicted stress, since our profession and our type of schools may well attract exactly those kinds of people to work in them, wonderful assets though they may be. At the other end of the spectrum, there may be some who need to learn to be more robust – and who need to be directly confronted with that fact. Maybe there is a similar correlation between those who complain the most and those who need to be told that they have the least to complain about.

We need therefore to know each one as an individual; to understand their individual circumstances; and to be able to 'flex' policies for individuals without losing consistency or fairness. Hence also the need to ensure that recruitment procedures identify the right people, those who will thrive and add value to the culture of our particular school, and to raise warning signs if this is not the case.

In my school, we are at pains to stress at interview what working in a full seven-day-a-week boarding school means, so that we can assess whether a candidate is right for us and vice versa, and we are constantly refining our recruitment processes to emphasise that fact. As managers we can much more easily teach skills to our employees than change their attitudes and personalities. We need to hire people who really 'get' the culture of our school.

Good induction and mentoring procedures are essential too, especially as we all make ambitious demands on colleagues from the moment of interview and appointment. This is especially true in their early years when they have to prepare every lesson meticulously *and* take on big new extracurricular loads. Part of the trick will be having the right people running the induction and mentoring programme so that feedback and support is available both to the new joiner and to the SMT (or one member of it) if someone is struggling. Moreover the SMT will need regularly to review how things are progressing at each stage of a colleague's career.

PGCE support and NQT induction is the start of it, but the list develops from there. It includes identifying and grasping issues in the early years, rather than leaving things unspoken or problems stored up for later on; guidance for all staff on the balance between empathy and courting popularity; particular pressures on those in their middle years, as HoDs or houseparents, with or without growing families of their own; finding fulfilling roles for those who have finished as a HoD or in a house but who have not gone on to be SMT members; support for SMT members themselves who are dealing with intense pressure and often soaking up moans and gripes; keeping people stimulated and afloat in their final years before retirement; handling the complexities of later retirement and requests for part-time work. So the list goes on.

The list is not exclusively related to teachers. Keep an eye also on the non-teaching staff. In most schools there will be a need to work towards a single school culture, even if there is always going to be something of a divide between academic and support staff for the simple reason that they do different kinds of jobs. But it is worth reflecting on ideas for encouraging a single school ethos.

Look out for opportunities for whole-staff events. When an inspection or similar event has gone really well, reward all colleagues equally with a good party, a one-off gift or bonus that is the same for the cleaners and gardeners as it is for the Head and bursar. The start of a new academic year provides an opportunity for the Head to address the whole staff (all employees) and give a brief state of the union message, followed perhaps by a short reception or snacks.

In dealing with inter-staff relationships between academic and support staff, it sends a strong signal if you insist on mutual respect regardless of roles and if you take clear action on any comments or behaviour that undermine that. This also has a ripple effect in terms of setting the example from staff to pupils: if pupils can see that teachers and support staff respect each other regardless of rank and role, they are more likely to do the same when they are interacting with caterers, cleaners and matrons in their houses, and much more likely to carry that ethos with them into the world beyond school, too.

Make sure the bursar gets out and about too and that s/he is practising MBWA as well as you. Have regular conversations (including in his/her appraisal) about who keeps an eye on the welfare of the non-teaching staff. And last, but by no means least important, make sure you know who keeps an eye on the wellbeing of the bursar and the Head.

The two can help each other in this respect if the working relationship is sufficiently strong and open, but there is a role too for your PA, deputy and others on the SMT, as well as of course your spouse. Make sure you develop your own strategies for spotting signs of overload in yourself and for managing it. If you are looking after others, you need to look after yourself.

Specialist training and agencies can also help everyone enormously. The chaplain has a critical role to play both in supporting the Head as a critical friend and pastoral/spiritual guide, and in providing support to colleagues in times of need. Many schools (including mine) engage the services of a professional counsellor too, and it is important that this support is available to staff as well as pupils. In times of trauma or tragedy or *in extremis*, be prepared to call in extra support including bereavement counselling or psychiatric help if need be.

All of these services will need to be coordinated by someone on the SMT, so that the left hand and the right hand know what each other is doing, whilst confidences are appropriately respected. In difficult times we shall need to be flexible over time off in lieu, or compassionate leave. In my experience colleagues are hugely grateful for such sensitivity and flexibility and in any case if the issue is urgent and significant they will not be much use at work unless it is granted. Equally, I can think of two or three instances in my own school recently when getting back to work and being supported flexibly over work patterns was essential to someone's recovery after a trauma or bereavement. The balance between the need for routines and the need for space is, again, a very individual one.

A well-timed bunch of flowers or box of chocolates, a handwritten card or personal note can be a great signal of care and concern for the individual and it is a good idea to set aside a moment each day to think about who might be in need of such a gesture – and to encourage SMT colleagues to let you know if they have spotted someone in need and feel that perhaps you haven't done so.

Everyone will have different approaches to Christmas cards for staff, but if time and the size of your common room allow, it is a great opportunity to write an encouraging personal comment on a specific thing you really appreciated about that person's contribution in the past year. If this is not possible every year, try it once every few years or at least pick out those who have really gone through the mill or gone way beyond the call of duty. Don't underestimate the impact of the personal touch. Always go to funerals.

One of the very best questions I was asked at a Headship interview was: "Where and when does pastoral care end?" In a similar vein I recall hearing an excellent talk by an experienced Head some years ago entitled: 'How many hands can you hold?' These questions take me back to that conversation which I had a decade ago on that North Carolina beach. They are as relevant to the pastoral care of staff as they are to that of our pupils. Unlike in a TV game show, they have no final answer. Each of us will develop different personal approaches, will inherit a different school culture and will be dealing with a different set of individuals. It's a remarkable privilege to be involved with so many lives and to listen to so many fascinating stories.

Chapter 10

Developing people and developing yourself

Melvyn Roffe

"I didn't get where I am today without..." In one of the original episodes of *The Rise and Fall of Reginald Perrin*, Reggie Perrin's boss, Charles Jefferson (C J), sacks Reggie, telling him: "I could practically destroy this firm if I started caring about people... I didn't get where I am today by caring about people."

Boarding schools are people-places. The success of a good boarding school lies not so much in the shininess of its buildings or even, some would argue, the glittering nature of the prizes gained by its pupils, but in the high quality of the professional relationship between staff and pupils (and, of course, between pupils themselves and between members of staff).

But boarding schools are also busy places and it is easy for the importance of developing boarding school people to be overshadowed or obscured by the tyranny of the timetable, the duty rota and the fixture list – and the exigencies of dealing with the crises great and small which inevitably arise during any term.

The job we do and the jobs that we lead others in doing are constantly changing and the demands on us and our schools are ever more complex. Without professional development we stand no chance of keeping up with and benefiting from the pace of change or of understanding how we can protect our schools from its less desirable aspects.

Developing new recruits
Whilst young teachers joining boarding schools today share many of the fine qualities of their counterparts who started, say, 20 years ago, they also show some significant differences. The chances that they have themselves

had a boarding school education may well be smaller. However dedicated they are to their job, they will expect a stronger work-life balance and they will want to know how their role will develop and what opportunities there will be to enable them to take the next step in their career progression.

If they have been recruited from a postgraduate certificate of education (or equivalent) course they will probably arrive in their first post with a formal statement of areas for development in their year as a newly qualified teacher (NQT). None of those will, however, relate explicitly to boarding. Today's graduates also see development, correctly, as an entitlement and may well look more favourably upon an employer who takes the fulfilment of that entitlement seriously.

The success of inducting and developing new recruits to the school, whether they are fresh from college in their early 20s, or are taking up teaching later in life, depends on a number of crucial factors. The induction programme itself should begin as soon as practical after appointment and new recruits should be made to feel part of the team from the outset. Any good induction programme will be a combination of formal sessions with people the member of staff needs to meet and subjects (for example child protection) which must be covered and a more informal introduction to the culture of the school. And yes, that should include the mores of the common room bar – if there is one.

Early familiarisation with boarding routines, procedures and expectations is also essential. Those whose understanding of the working of a boarding house has been drawn mainly from the works of J K Rowling need, literally, to see and feel what the inside of a boarding house is like. Those who have experience as a boarder themselves will nevertheless need to see the experience anew from the adult perspective.

Crucial to the success of new boarding staff will be their ability rapidly to strike the delicate balance between firmness and approachability that is always needed in dealing with boarders – and to understand the often subtle but always important ways in which the relationship between teachers and pupils is different in a boarding house from that in a classroom. Here participation in one of the Boarding Schools' Association (BSA) courses designed for new boarding staff may be helpful.

In the early months, the new recruit should know and understand the nature of the development upon which he or she is embarked through the induction programme. There should be a carefully chosen mentor: perhaps, but not necessarily, the housemaster/housemistress or head of boarding who will not only dispense wisdom and counsel when required but will also encourage the new recruit to reflect on their development and put both problems and successes into context.

This first phase in the career of a member of the boarding staff will probably be the most crucial of all and much future success or failure will flow from it. Expectations and anxiety may both be high and they will both need to be managed. Workload must also be monitored carefully if the new recruit is to stand a reasonable chance of making a strong start in his or her chosen career; of meeting the standards expected by the school and of enjoying the experience of working in a boarding school.

All professional development activity can be characterised in one of three ways. It is either activity designed to help you do your current job better, or activity designed to prepare you for the next job that you will do, or activity intended more broadly to develop you as a professional person. Most staff will benefit from all three types of development, and new recruits are no exception to this.

Whilst there are plenty of external courses designed for new entrants to the profession, most schools have excellent opportunities for development to occur within the school itself, if they did but realise it. Not only is this logistically and financially beneficial, but it also enables the school to benefit directly by extending the contribution made by a new member of staff. Staff in large schools in particular benefit by seeing areas and aspects of the school that they may not otherwise get to know, and by working with a broader range of colleagues.

Examples of 'professional development by doing' might include a new member of staff being appointed to assist the educational visits co-ordinator, or to develop an aspect of the school's international visits or community service programme. Opportunities within the Combined Cadet Force should clearly be recognised by the school as professional development, as should activities supported by one of the national governing bodies for sport.

Younger members of staff may be more tuned in than their older colleagues to the way in which today's students use technology, as well as its potential both for learning and abuse; thus they may be able to make particular contributions to the development of e-learning.

As well as work within the department, new colleagues might be encouraged to undertake a particular development activity, looking at some aspect of learning across departments and reporting back to more senior colleagues. This 'action research' approach to professional development is very much at the heart of the BSA/Roehampton Institute accredited courses for boarding staff and there is a great deal of evidence of the benefits that have been derived both by staff and schools from the work that has been done.

Depending on the individual, a new member of staff with previous business experience of project management or marketing, for example, might make an invaluable contribution to those aspects within the school. However, there can sometimes be dangers in mixing current and former professional responsibilities in this way – at least, before the new arrival is fully tuned in to the needs and levels of understanding of pupils.

New colleagues in schools with a strongly hierarchical culture may find it difficult to contribute ideas and understanding unless there is clear sanction and support given by the Head and senior team. One approach might be to create temporary posts with a title such as 'research associate', and to provide written and verbal opportunities for research findings to be disseminated. It should be clear from the outset that any recommendations may or may not be implemented within the school, but even if this proves to be the case, the research should be valued as part of the professional discourse within the school to which all staff are invited to contribute.

Blogs and chat-rooms within the school's virtual learning environment (VLE) may provide less formal (but still useful) forums for the exchange and development of ideas. Appointing an official 'ginger group' of research associates reporting to the senior team may be a good way not only of developing staff but also of clearing barriers to the improvement of the school.

Heads should always have a clear view of how their own routine management decisions affect professional development opportunities for staff. Are staff allocated permanently to specific boarding houses, for example, or is there the opportunity (or expectation) that they will move to experience different types of house and different styles of leadership from housemasters and housemistresses?

Perhaps most importantly, it should be clear how the school's performance management procedures support real professional development. An effective performance management system will lead on naturally and seamlessly from the initial induction programme and will encourage staff to develop a habit of self reflection and self improvement. It should not become, or be seen as, merely an instrument of management control (although on occasion it may have also to be that).

Ideally, performance management should also provide opportunities for colleagues to develop themselves within the system, for example as peer mentors and coaches. These opportunities are perhaps of particular value to colleagues whose professional development is not focused on moving up the management ladder, but on developing their own ability to do their current job better. Experienced and successful classroom teachers, given 'permission' by the performance management system to observe and work with other classroom colleagues can often improve not only the performance of the colleague with whom they are working, but also their own practice. The same must be true of boarding practitioners.

Developing middle leaders

Most schools will have a variety of 'middle leaders', usually known collectively as 'middle management'. Some, but probably not all, will have titles and management allowances. Anyone who has a degree of responsibility for someone's work other than their own can be considered a middle leader. In many boarding schools this middle leadership will comprise both heads of department and heads of boarding houses, with the relationship between the two groups often being the most crucial one in the school. In larger schools with fewer boarders, the boarding management structure may be separate from the main structures of the school – arguably increasing the need for sound professional development for boarding staff.

Again, external providers including the BSA will undoubtedly play a role in staff development. An important aspect of the school gaining full benefit from the considerable cost (not to mention disruption to lessons and boarding duties) of staff going away on courses or conferences is to ensure that there are ways in which the benefit can be shared after the return of the participant. Reports from courses and associated materials uploaded onto the school intranet or VLE can be an easy way of doing this. However, time should also be afforded within appropriate staff meetings for short presentations on the subjects covered. Major issues can also be covered in this way during whole school continuing professional development (CPD) or INSET days.

The advantage of this is not only to save the cost of an external speaker. Well-informed home grown presenters almost always seem to be more effective than all but the most exceptional outsiders on such occasions. They know their audience better; are less likely to make controversial solecisms and can better adapt the subject matter to the individual circumstances of the school. New ideas are perhaps more readily accepted from one of one's own, and there is a resident expert to whom to turn later. Moreover the preparation and delivery of the presentation itself is excellent professional development for the serving or aspiring middle leader.

Dedicated and effective middle leaders run the risk of becoming encapsulated within the walls of their own fiefdoms: so focused on the routine success of their departments or houses that they fail to take care of their own needs, or the wider needs of the school. Reciprocal visits to other houses or departments, or houses or departments in other schools, participation as an Independent Schools Inspectorate (ISI) inspector, Ofsted Boarding Sector Additional Inspector (BSAI) or tutor with a local Initial Teacher Training (ITT) provider or the BSA accredited course can all help to overcome this tendency towards isolationism. And again, the benefits are by no means all one way.

Within the school, development for middle leaders should encourage them to see their role as more than mere petitioners seeking the patronage of the Head for their particular interest within the school. As in most things, healthy competition is a spur to improvement, but a collegiate approach to middle management within the school is likely to prove more effective overall.

To achieve this, middle leaders should be expected to do more than simply manage their own budgets, staff and material space (although it is important that they should be expected to do this well, too). Their development must also improve their capacity to see how their role fits within the overall objectives of the school – and what they can do to reach those objectives. And nowhere is that more important than in boarding schools where the differences between the regimes in boarding houses are frequently the source of, at very least, animated discussion.

Developing support staff

With the exception of the bursar, the senior teams of most schools consist solely of teachers. Small wonder then, that the development needs of support staff are sometimes overlooked, or are limited to specific training to meet health and safety or accreditation requirements. However, it would ideally be clear to all staff that their contribution to the wider success of the school and its pupils is welcomed, valued, developed and recognised. This is certainly essential in boarding schools where pupils are routinely in the care of staff who are not teachers. Whilst structures, timing and other details of development opportunities for support staff will often have to be different from those provided for teachers, the emphasis, structure and priority afforded them should be no different.

Developing the next generation of Heads

Schools in both the independent and state sectors seem certain to find increasing difficulty in attracting Heads of the right calibre over the next few years. The reasons for this are both demographic and attributable to the increased complexity and stress of the job. Most of the Heads of tomorrow are already working in schools today, so Heads should be doing what they can to secure the supply of those who will ultimately succeed them. Part of that will be to value and develop their own deputies – often the most difficult people to lose to attend a course or a conference because their absence will almost always coincide with a crisis which only the deputy is equipped to deal with.

The very least we can do, in addition to ensuring that our deputy does indeed get out of school every now and again, is to have an unwritten policy which ensures that deputies have experience of all the responsibilities of Headship – whether directly, by delegation or by some kind of job shadowing. The only risk of such an approach might be that it would further reduce the supply of candidates putting themselves forward for headship!

Deputies – and potentially other senior staff, too – may be considering the place of formal qualifications in their own development. It is now a requirement in the state sector that all those wishing to be appointed to headship should have the National Professional Qualification for Headship (NPQH) before taking up their first post. This is available (at a cost) to aspiring Heads in the independent sector and the sector itself is deliberating about how to provide a more appropriate equivalent to the NPQH and how to provide for independent schools the services provided in the state sector by the National College for Leadership of Schools and Children's Services (formerly NCSL).

National College courses, along with the Master of Business Administration (MBA) courses specific to education which are offered by many universities (for example Nottingham, De Montfort and Lincoln), provide a structured and academically rigorous form of professional development which, crucially, allows the degree of detachment from the routine rigours of school life and the opportunity for professional dialogue with experienced tutors and peers from other schools and sectors.

With busy terms and tight budgets it will never be possible for all school staff who would benefit from these courses to participate, but where it is not possible, it is all the more incumbent on schools to provide adequate other opportunities for development to occur. Appraisal by an experienced outsider might well be one example; the Head who appointed, and who has subsequently formed a close working relationship with a deputy aspiring to Headship, may now be too close to judge his or her strengths and weaknesses with the complete objectivity that a new pair of eyes can bring to the exercise.

Developing yourself if you are already a Head

And what, finally, of Heads themselves? How do we ensure that we develop our skills and experience; that we ourselves are enabled both to do our present job better and eventually to move on (if we wish to, and when the time is right) to another job in the future; that we develop the professional (and personal) hinterland upon which we draw routinely in discharging our responsibilities?

The principles of professional development for Heads should be no different from those for other staff. Development should be seen as an entitlement; it should be part of an acknowledged programme and should be related (but not entirely driven by) strong and supportive performance management. Additionally, there should generally be clear, tangible benefits to both the individual and the school which flow from the professional development activity.

There is likely to be a mix of training from outside providers and less formal opportunities which, for Heads, might include visits to and governance of other schools, involvement with professional bodies or universities or participation with Heads' networks, both real and virtual via the internet. A wise and supportive chairman of governors has a big part to play in this.

It has become accepted practice for governing bodies to appoint outside consultants to conduct Heads' appraisals. In the state sector, it is part of the role of the school improvement partner (SIP). Such appraisals should be the opportunity for the Head to identify his or her own needs for development in all areas of the job and to legitimise the spending of money and time by the Head on that development without guilt or fear of censure from governors or others.

To lead a good school, above all a good boarding school, we must care about people and their development. But to do our job properly we must also care for ourselves.

Chapter 11

Nursing and pastoral care

Kathy Compton

This chapter aims to show how nurses employed by independent schools, boarding and day, prep and senior, large or small, can be involved as an integral part of the school's pastoral care system.

First, at the risk of stating the obvious, schools vary hugely in the degree of medical back-up which they enjoy and can provide. On one hand, a large, rural boarding school may well have a medical unit containing several beds (although probably not the huge wards and operating theatre that some schools had in the epidemic-ridden days of former times); full-time staffing in term time; and very close liaison with the team of local doctors, one of whom acts as the school's medical officer, visiting the school on a daily basis. In smaller boarding schools, visits are perhaps once or twice a week.

By contrast, some day schools have no school doctor as the pupils will be registered with a variety of local practices. The link with a local doctor and surgery may be less formalised, and contact less frequent, but in these situations the nurses are very much on their own, and the support they receive can be a valuable resource for information and support for the nurse. The surgery or doctor can act as the link between the school and the local Health Protection Agency (HPA) if or when, for example, pandemic flu breaks out.

Precise arrangements as to who will liaise with the local HPA over any notifiable diseases will vary from school to school. The nurse will know which diseases fall into this category, and the HPA will support the school. However, it is the nurse who will be in the front line, involved with the senior management team in drawing up an appropriate policy to minimise any risk. Coherent emergency planning and clear lines of communication are essential in such circumstances. Guidance can be found for such a policy on the Teachernet, DoH, and DCSF websites.

Secondly, some factual and administrative issues. At present nurses go through an intensive three-year degree course to become qualified, then register with the Nursing and Midwifery Council (NMC) in order to be legally able to practice as nurses in Great Britain. Nurses from abroad also need to register with the NMC before working as nurses in this country. In order to remain on the register, a nurse needs to update her practice according to the current Post Regulation Education and Practice (PREP) regulations and – at present – to re-register every three years.

Schools should check annually that their nurses are registered with the NMC. Misconduct or bad practice by not following the NMC code may lead to de-registration. This ensures that nurses remain up-to-date and follow good working practices. It should be a concern that an independent school could in theory make a perfect place for a de-registered nurse to work. It is therefore essential that the checks with the NMC are made and registration sustained.

Nurses employed by independent schools often have no background in school nursing. They will have a variety of experience and qualifications gained after qualifying as nurses. Wherever possible, schools should endeavour to employ nurses who have backgrounds in children's nursing, A and E, practice nursing, or school nursing itself.

Nurses in our schools fulfil varied and extensive roles. According to the type of school – day or boarding, age range of the pupils, size of the school and number of nurses employed, the job description can be quite diverse. Most nurses will carry out the following:

- Conducting surgeries.
- Extensive record keeping.
- Administration of medicines both over the counter and prescribed.
- Overseeing the care of pupils with chronic illnesses.
- Dealing with accidents, including sports injuries.
- Overseeing rehabilitation after accidents and sports injuries.
- Providing a listening service for both pupils and staff.
- Carrying out health checks.

- Giving or arranging for immunisation programmes and/or travel vaccinations.

- Managing a budget, ordering stock and supplies.

- Linking the school to outside health resources, *eg* Child and Adolescent Mental Health Services (CAMHS), local surgery, local Primary Care Trust (PCT) school nurses.

- Advising on sex and relationship issues, drugs including smoking.

Within the school, nurses should be:

- Involved in writing medical policies and protocols.

- Involved in writing whole school policies where applicable.

- Working in teams/committees, *eg* organising case conferences for pupils with mental health issues (self harm, eating disorders).

- Collating information on pupils whom staff have identified as having pastoral concerns.

- Involved in safeguarding issues.

- Involved with the health and safety issues.

- Teaching first aid to staff and pupils.

- Teaching support staff on medical issues.

- Teaching and advising on the PSHE curriculum.

- Health promotion.

As this list shows, the nurse's job is not simply a matter of practicalities and administration. It contributes an important – even unique – component in a school's overall pastoral care, because it brings the nurse into contact with pupils in a wide variety of ways – not least, as the frequently used first point of contact by those with troubled minds.

The nurse is often available at times when teaching staff may not be around. It is important just to listen to pupils: they may come on a pretext – to test the water before opening up and talking about an issue that is causing them either passing or more deeply-rooted concern. Nurses can often spot these pupils and persuade them to discuss the 'real' issue behind the visit. They may also have more time than their academic colleagues.

As a result, the nurse is often in a privileged position of being uniquely in receipt of highly personal information from pupils. However, the extent to which such confidences can be shared within the school is an important and complex issue: how much of the information given to the nursing staff can be shared? And at this point we need to distinguish between two often-confused ideas: confidentiality and consent. Both of these involve the Fraser guidelines, dealing with so-called Gillick competence (see www.patient.co.uk/doctor/Consent-to-Treatment-in-Children.htm).

Confidentiality is often misunderstood, but can become a real issue between the nurse and her teaching colleagues within the school. Protecting *any* patient's right to confidentiality – in this case, the student's – is an obligation for nurses under the code laid down by their governing body, the NMC. In order to remain registered, a nurse cannot break this code, which is explicit in summarising what is expected:

- You must respect people's right to confidentiality.
- You must ensure people are informed about how and why information is shared by those who will be providing their care.
- You must disclose information if you believe someone may be at risk of harm, in line with the law of the country in which you are practising.

This is where nurses can sometimes find themselves in very difficult situations. Teachers are not bound by such tight restrictions in their professional lives, but every nurse is responsible under the NMC code for her own actions. Thus a nurse working alone in a school without medical line management (this will be discussed later) may find making a decision alone causes teaching colleagues to regard him or her as being at best awkward and at worst obstructive. It should therefore be remembered that although employed by the school, the nurse's clear obligation is to the pupil, not to the school.

The NMC code's Confidential Guidelines (May 2008) make three other assertions:

> Sometimes nurses and midwives may be under pressure to release information. They will be held accountable for any disclosure they

make. The nurse or midwife must justify his or her decision to deliberately release information deemed to be in the best interests of the public.

There is no statutory right to confidentiality, but an aggrieved individual can sue through a civil court, alleging that confidentiality was broken.

Nurses and midwives who decide to disclose confidential information without consent should do so only in exceptional circumstances. They should be able to justify their actions. Disclosure without consent is done only in the public interest to protect individuals, groups or society as a whole from the risk of significant harm. Examples could include child abuse, serious crime or drug trafficking.

It will be clear by now that a certain amount of common sense by those working in the school has to be used with this issue, whilst remaining within the law. The school should have a clear confidentiality policy agreed by those who will be affected by it. This should provide guidelines on scenarios *before* anyone comes face to face with them.

Where there is not 24-hour medical cover in a boarding school, for example, it would be irresponsible for a nurse not to pass on that a pupil had been unwell during the day, or had received medication. Once the pupils are made aware that this is a school policy for illnesses such as injuries, colds, temperatures, toothache – in other words, things that will probably continue as problems after the medical centre is shut – there is usually no problem in sharing that information with the house staff who will be continuing that pupil's care.

Similarly, where a pupil has been unwell overnight in the boarding house this information should be shared with medical staff coming on duty in the morning. It is useful for the medical centre to be given a daily update in order to keep individual pupil records up-to-date.

However, where a pupil specifically does not give permission for information to be passed on, it would be quite wrong for a nurse to pass this on to the parents, guardians or house staff, unless the above NMC criteria (permitting the passing on of information) were fulfilled. At the same time, the nurse will be trying to persuade the pupil to talk to his or her parent, guardian or house staff.

These situations often arise about contraception issues, other sexual matters or alcohol or drug misuse. For example, a girl under the age of 16 taking the pill may not wish either her parents or the boarding staff to know. She may be taking it for medical reasons and will not want staff to 'get the wrong idea'. There is no significant medical risk in this situation, and providing that the nurse is totally confident that there is no child protection issue, this can be kept confidential. However, the nurse and prescribing doctor will assess the girl's suitability and maturity using the Fraser Guidelines. They will also be discussing with the pupil why the contraception is necessary, giving guidance on its use and trying to persuade the girl to talk to her parents about the whole issue. Issues around the age of consent to be involved in a sexual act are discussed below.

Sometimes a pupil's need for confidentiality would be understood by any layman who was party to the information. For example, I have had personal experience of working with a pupil who was given a *stoma* (an artificial opening on the abdomen following surgery, to collect waste in a reservoir bag). He was terribly embarrassed about this and specifically asked the Head to ensure that no one be told. In order for him to be able to change and empty his bag in a private area, should it be needed during the day, it was agreed that the medical centre should also know.

When it became apparent that he was going to take part in an expedition on Dartmoor for his Duke of Edinburgh's Award, agreement was reached that enabled us to tell the member of staff in charge of the expedition. Facilities were arranged for the pupil at the school Outward Bound Centre. The arrangement was clearly on a 'need to know' basis, and every step of the sharing of information was agreed with the pupil and his parents.

Another unusual case was that of a 16 year-old girl, diagnosed with a *prolactinoma*. This tumour on her pituitary gland manifested itself through causing her to lactate. She was naturally very embarrassed by this and felt that people would regard her differently, should they know. Once diagnosed, a simple treatment of a tablet taken once a week brought the tumour under control. She was desperate for no one within the school to be told of her condition, and as she wasn't in any danger and quite capable of looking after and administering the medication herself, no one was told. She had been persuaded to involve her mother. In most situations a nurse will try to persuade a pupil that their parents and/or house staff should be informed. However, the nurse is not always successful, and *the patient has the last word.*

When talking to a BSA Heads' conference, a school medical officer (MO) cited a situation where a parent demanded to know why he was paying on the school bill for a consultant's bill and 'matron's runs' (*ie* car journeys), assuming that he was not 'sponsoring someone for the marathon'! In this particular instance, the case concerned a divorced family: although the mother was in the picture, the father was not. The MO spoke to the boy and sought his written permission to write to the father with a report of the situation.

Then there is the issue of consent. It, too, can cause real concerns. Essentially, it is up to the nurse or doctor to establish that if a pupil is under the age of 16 s/he is competent to make a decision for him or herself. The NMC has consent guidelines as follows:

> Children under the age of 16 are generally considered to lack the capacity to consent or to refuse treatment. The right to do so remains with the parents, or those with parental responsibility, unless the child is considered to have significant understanding and intelligence to make up his or her own mind about it.
>
> Children of 16 or 17 are presumed to be able to consent for themselves, although it is considered good practice to involve the parents. Parents or those with parental responsibility may override the refusal of a child of any age up to 18 years. In exceptional circumstances, it may be necessary to seek an order from the court.
>
> Child minders, teachers and other adults caring for the child cannot normally give consent.

This last statement is important: house staff cannot give consent for a pupil to receive medical treatment. Guidelines from a Department of Health publication, July 2001, entitled *Consent – what you have a right to expect – a guide for children and young people* are also relevant to this:

When can you give consent for yourself?
Always if you are 16-18 years old.

You can give consent to being examined or treated in the same way that adults can. If you agree to a particular treatment, the doctor or nurse does not have to ask your parents for consent as well. But if you decide to refuse a particular treatment, sometimes your parents may get involved.

Sometimes if you are under 16.

If you are under 16, you may still be able to give consent for yourself – provided you're able to understand what is involved in the proposed treatment.

Consent issues arise (for example) within schools over vaccinations where a pupil may not want a vaccination and the parent may wish the child to have it, or vice versa. The most often-publicised situation involving consent occurs where a girl under 16 wants the contraceptive pill, and the fact that that under 16 it is technically illegal for a girl to be involved in a sexual act. Whatever the pros and cons of being seen to condone early sexual activity in young people, here we run into the ethically difficult area of what might be termed 'the lesser evil' – to ignore the law, or to protect the teenager against an unwanted pregnancy.

Some practitioners take the view that the latter consideration should override the former, as long as there is no safeguarding issue. Under the age of 13, sexual activity is regarded as a serious safeguarding issue. Under Fraser guidelines contraception can be given at the doctor's discretion. The doctor would also follow local safeguarding procedures.

In many schools the nurse will facilitate the provision of the 'morning after pill'. This should be prescribed for each pupil requiring it by a doctor and a stock should not be kept and issued by the nurse. Day pupils can be prescribed any contraceptive by a doctor who is not their own GP. Where this service is available it should be mentioned in a relevant school policy so that parents are aware of it.

Given all the complexities of these issues, it is very important that the nurse feels that the house staff can be trusted to keep sensitive information confidential. This is a two-way process. However careful and sensitive people are, confidentiality will continue to create problems of misunderstanding in schools. But I hope that I have gone some way to explain exactly why nurses can appear to be obstructive about not sharing information. A specific policy written by those involved should go some way to preventing misunderstandings.

Meanwhile there are some important issues of communication. Communication can be further obstructed when nurses find themselves simply on the wrong administrative list within a school. Many schools have the bursar as the line manager for the medical staff because nurses come under the 'non-teaching staff' heading. However, a nurse's job is entirely focused on the pupils' welfare; therefore any information about pupils which is being disseminated through the school staff should also go to the nurses. So often, information goes to the teaching staff but people forget to inform the nurses. If the bursar is to be line manager, it is also important that whoever is responsible for passing pastoral information on to the teachers is made aware that the nurses also need to know. In order to operate effectively, it is essential that nurses are given access to all systems within the school. They need to be able to contact parents easily and should therefore have access to the school's information system and also email, fax and phone. However, as already noted, their own record-keeping systems should be confidential.

It is helpful if the school's nurse is invited to staff meetings so that information can be properly and appropriately shared. Ideally, the nurse is fully 'in the know' about what is happening in the coming week, and about specific or general pastoral concerns which teaching staff may have about pupils. The staff meeting is an opportunity for the nurse to keep colleagues informed, at least in a general way, even if no specifics are possible, about issues that a pupil may have which might be affecting performance in class or with homework.

Similarly close liaison is important with boarding staff: if there is a weekly staff meeting for them, the nurse should attend. If the pupil has approved, specific information can be passed on; if not, general concerns may be raised so that boarding staff are more alert. Even if the confidentiality rules prevent full disclosure, keeping the lines of communication as open as possible within a boarding community is an essential part of caring for children away from home.

The mental health policy at the school where I work names the medical centre as responsible for collating information about pupils who are self harming, or who have an eating disorder or any other mental health worry. We have found over the years that in situations such as these, pupils tend to take a member of staff into their confidence, then move on to another member of staff – who could be teaching, medical or support staff. Unless there is a system of co-ordination, these pupils can get progressively worse as they move from one staff member to the next. It is well known that the sooner a mental health issue is treated the better the outcome. A mental health issue is also likely to cause tremendous pressure in the pupil's peer group. It is made clear through our PSHE sessions that the nurses will always listen to a pupil who is having problems 'helping' a friend. A friend's loyalty and wish to stay silent can be misguided when self-harm and eating disorders are concerned.

Isolation is an issue for nurses in independent schools and the lack of information both from school and in general on relevant nursing issues can cause best practice not to be followed. It is in the school's interest that their nurses are up-to-date. The nurse's problem is that if they don't know the information is out there, they don't look for it.

One way around this is for the school to commission the local Primary Care Trust (PCT) to supervise the nurse and to pass on information that comes to it on issues related to school nursing and children and young people. This will give the school access to a number of systems that will help with the pastoral care within the school. Nurses must keep up-to-date in order to remain registered with the NMC. It is therefore essential that they are able to attend relevant study days, both local and national. The Boarding Schools' Association runs training specifically for nurses working in a boarding context. The Royal College of Nursing and the Medical Officers in Schools Association also run study days and conferences that are specifically for independent school nurses.

Nurses should be involved in the variety of committees that exist within our schools: the health and safety committee, pastoral care committee, year group meetings, and safeguarding meetings will all benefit from the participation of the nurse. From their training and links with outside organisations, nurses can bring a lot of information and experience to these meetings. Nurses working in independent schools do have access to the PCT safeguarding nurse, and should have their details readily available in case of safeguarding concerns. They should of course also follow school policy and report their concerns to the school's Child Protection safeguarding officer.

They also have an important role to play in liaising with anyone brought in to provide medical cover for rugby matches. They should be involved with the PE staff (and, in some schools, the doctor) in ensuring that adequate cover is provided. The way that this is achieved varies from the nurses standing on the touchline supported by the school doctor, to the nurses staying in the medical centre, to the school employing physiotherapists, first-aiders or paramedics. In some schools agency nurses may be employed but it is essential that the school ensures that whoever is giving cover is correctly trained. Nurses and doctors do not necessarily make good first-aiders, as their training mostly involves equipment that may not be available on a touchline.

There is no doubt that nurses can, and indeed should, have a central role within the pastoral care system in a school. They are a useful resource to teaching and boarding staff for information on how to deal with difficult issues. They have excellent background knowledge on many issues. They have access to outside links which can be contacted to help where difficulties arise. Most keep excellent records of pupil visits which may be able to throw light on to issues.

Pupils will often opt to talk to the medical staff even about non-medical issues. When necessary, pupils can usually be persuaded to allow the nurse to talk to the relevant staff member so that the issue can be resolved. Parents respect the nursing staff for their professional background and knowledge on medical matters and are almost always happy to involve them in pastoral care situations.

In short, the nurses in your schools are professional people with up-to-date qualifications and wide-ranging experience, a very long way from being no more than glorified first-aiders. They are a valuable resource to any school as it sets out to care for both day and boarding pupils. In the best schools, with systems and communications structures in place, and with senior management support, they are vital, integral members of the pastoral team.

Chapter 12

Head of the sixth form

James Priory

In the same week in 2009 that Portsmouth welcomed home 17 year-old Mike Perham, the youngest person to sail solo around the world, a Dutch court placed a 13 year-old girl in state care to prevent her bid to circumnavigate the globe. Instead of tackling 50-foot waves and gale force winds, Laura Dekker found herself back in the classroom and at the centre of a debate about how, both culturally and legally, we define childhood. What is the appropriate age for a young person to be free to take the physical and psychological risks inherent in a global challenge?

Any sixth form worth its sea salt has to engage with this same tension and strike a workable balance between encouraging its members to take risks and become independent whilst observing the community's rules and modelling best behaviour for other pupils in the school. The decision as to whether to call your sixth formers pupils or students, with all the connotations that these terms imply, can be revealing – and tantalising too, if you recognise that they will probably be a curious hybrid of the two.

The rite of passage which two years in the sixth form represents is not dissimilar to the three months in which Jane Austen's Emma, for all her confidence and ostentatious reading lists, must learn to read the world around her as she prepares for her 21st birthday and adulthood. Cleverness and wisdom, as Austen wryly reminds us, are very different qualities indeed. And there can be a world of difference between someone who is 16 and that same person two years later.

When I became head of sixth form, I was encouraged to develop Years 12 and 13, not as a school within a school, but as a college within a school. In an area where almost all maintained secondary schools finish at 16 and state school pupils move on to large sixth form colleges, the challenge to retain and recruit pupils into our own sixth form lay in combating their perception that the grass must surely be greener where there is no uniform, no morning registration, and freedom is apparently boundless.

Whilst pupils may feel ready for life on the high seas, however, their parents are often concerned by the diminishing currency of high Cs in a congested university market. The school sixth form is seen as offering reassuring support structures; academic expertise in shortage subject areas; a distinguished track record in university applications. In short, it is the reliability of what the school sixth form offers which can appeal to parents whilst appalling the more free-spirited pupils coming to the end of their GCSEs.

But there is danger in underestimating the maturity of 16 year-olds, who will be well aware that what is on offer is to their benefit, if they wish to secure a passport to the university of their choice. 'Career' is an unfortunate choice of word for the idea of a progressive journey through life. Buzz Lightyear puts it nicely in *Toy Story 2* when he shouts to Woody, as the pair make a dramatic escape through an open window, "This isn't flying, this is falling with style!" Very few of your pupils will really wish to be a second Icarus, however much they rebel against codes of conduct and restrictive rules of school life. Parents will also wish to be cautious if their son or daughter fails to feel excited by what your sixth form has on offer.

One of the solutions that my own school has found powerful has been to think about where our young people will be when they are 25 and not simply about what grades they will have in their hands as they walk out of the school at 18. Taking a longer view helps to encourage pupils to keep their options open with regard to university and career choices: taking care not to close doors unnecessarily, in rejecting what Boris Johnson likes to call 'crunchy' subjects after GCSE. But it also signals our interest in ensuring that their sixth-form experience equips them well for life beyond university. Something, no doubt, Buzz Lightyear could express in a suitable catchphrase.

As Headmaster I have inherited a tradition of interviewing all pupils in Year 11 where I ask them precisely that question: "Where do you want to be when you are 25 and how can we help you to get there?" Not everyone has an answer and personally I am still considering my own response. But many do, and their ideas help enormously in shaping the sixth-form courses, trips, taster experiences, visiting speaker programmes and career mentoring we offer.

It is a question we also ask of those interested in joining us from outside, whether they are coming from a local state school and are keen to weigh up what an independent school sixth form has to offer or whether they are simply interested in a change of environment.

Despite the perception fuelled in the press that some universities favour candidates applying from a state school background, it has been very encouraging to see external recruitment grow markedly in recent years. This raises the challenge of how well your school can support pupils new to the school in settling into a large and dynamic sixth form where the majority of the year group already know each other well, some since they were in Reception and scurrying around at ankle height further years ago.

Most schools have developed excellent induction programmes into the sixth form. These may include early invitations to information evenings or subject forums held at the school during Year 11, as well as taster days and induction events in the summer term post GCSE.

Residential weekends away with other pupils joining the sixth form can also be successful, providing an opportunity for team building.

Schools often find it helpful to hold an induction day at the end of the summer for everyone preparing to start Year 12. This has the practical advantage of being able to resolve option changes and timetabling issues, but it is also a chance for the sixth-form team to set the tone for the start of the academic year and a great opportunity for pupils and staff to socialise, lighting the rusting barbecue in defiant farewell to the sizzling summer that never was.

In some ways, the challenges faced by pupils joining your school at 16+ are not dissimilar to those facing pupils who are making the transition from Year 11 in a school with which they are already familiar. The step-up to A level or IB, for example, can be daunting for some, if liberating for others: greater exposure in smaller sets; the pace and complexity of university-standard material; renewed emphasis on independent learning, which probably means a less rigid homework structure and habits of research and enquiry that the scaffolding of GCSE rarely require.

However, for pupils joining you from a smaller school or from an environment in which expectations have been less demanding, the challenge to establish themselves in a new year group at breakneck speed could be overwhelming. Many schools offer bursaries specifically aimed at the sixth form and this can also mean that pupils who have never been in a private school before can suddenly feel like fish out of water. So you have to take thoughtful action to minimise those risks.

My own experience has taught me not to generate unnecessary apprehension in this situation. It is important that pupils, parents and staff understand that, academically, pupils new to the sixth form are unlikely to be all-singing-all-dancing right at the start of the course. Establish realistic expectations and goals, and pupils will feel that they are making progress. Appoint sixth-form buddies or peer mentors. Encourage involvement in at least two different co-curricular activities by the time of the October half term. Unless there are specific concerns needing action, avoid the temptation to hold too many review meetings too early, in case you run the risk of undermining the confidence that motivated the pupil to come to you in the first place.

As head of sixth form, you will have played a major part in recruiting and, indeed, retaining pupils into your sixth form. You want the best for them and you want the best from them, having articulated with integrity and passion what makes your school the ideal place in which for them to spend two critical years of their lives.

The challenge for you, especially if your sixth form is a large one, can be to recognise that each pupil's day-to-day experience will be determined by factors that are partly out of your immediate control, but nonetheless part of your wider responsibility, given your uniquely academic and pastoral role: the quality of teaching and learning; the culture of the sixth-form centre; and most important of all, the care and support of their tutor.

It is the tutor who must play a central role and any complacency here can be costly for the individual pupil and the reputation of your sixth form. If Isaac Newton had lived a little longer, he might have established a rule of gravity for heads of department becoming sixth-form tutors: that the academic apple rises rather than falls in the pastoral orchard.

It is entirely natural for HoDs to gravitate to the sixth form where they can share their subject expertise, as well as their wider knowledge of university and careers. HoDs can make fine tutors, respected by their pupils as subject gurus and authoritative figures in the academic life of the school; but you should also be prepared to expect – and some time have to demand – a high quality of tutoring from *all* of your team. There is an equally valid argument that a school benefits from having HoDs tutoring across the age range.

An effective sixth-form tutor should have the confidence and freedom to develop his or her own rapport with the group. Tutors may need to be given encouragement, for example, to organise tutor group social outings, such as a trip to the cinema or a restaurant meal. They need to be able to create an atmosphere of trust, learning to hear what is said – and not said – in those informal day-to-day chats: insights into tensions at home; hints about too much time spent socialising or in a job outside school; fraying relationships with a particular member of staff; low self-esteem in a subject or activity. All these things will have significance in supporting their tutees' wellbeing and academic progress.

Tutors also have a role as advocates of their tutees in times of trouble. But championing their tutees' talents and achievements should not prevent them from being able to scrutinise their academic performance and behaviour as well. A strong tutor should be able to express concern and disappointment as well as delight and affirmation, earning the respect as well as affection of all sixth-form tutees over time.

An early phone call home by the tutor is helpful in establishing a relationship with parents who need to feel assured that there is a point of contact for them, even though their child is entering the most mature phase of his or her school life. Email is another well-established tool for parents and tutors to stay in touch with each other. Giving parents an opportunity early in the school year to come and meet their son's or daughter's tutor is also time well spent.

There are many ways to ensure that you get the best from your team of tutors. Visiting tutor groups to catch up with individual pupils is a natural opportunity to gather a flavour of what is happening in tutor time. More formally, you can observe tutor sessions or even carry out some team tutoring: delivering PSHE topics, jointly with the tutor. Tutors need to see other tutors at work, too. Enabling tutor groups to come together for activities is an opportunity for this, whether for social and charitable events or for simple administrative purposes. Pairings of tutors can work well, encouraging colleagues to share approaches and resources. Tutor groups belonging to a house system, day or boarding, can be another way of developing professional liaison between colleagues.

As well as having a traditional day house system in which heads of house oversee groups of children vertically mixed up to Year 13, we also have a horizontal system of heads of year. This includes the head of sixth form and a dedicated team of deputy heads of year and specialist co-ordinators of areas such as university admissions.

Given Portsmouth's nautical setting, there is a comforting sense of longitude and latitude for my colleagues and me in mapping a pupil's situation and progress in this way. To avoid the danger of crossed lines and mixed messages, however, it is even more important that the tutor remains the first point of contact for parents – an active figure at the centre of the school's pastoral life. We have a regular pastoral and academic review meeting chaired by the head of sixth form which focuses on each house on a weekly rotation and which is attended by the tutors so that they can talk about the progress of their tutees.

INSET dedicated to sharing best practice can also be effective, perhaps offered as twilight sessions. Ensure, too, that pastoral performance is given due attention in your continuous professional development and appraisal system. Giving pupils the opportunity to provide constructive feedback on their tutor group experience is also as valuable as ensuring pupils are able to comment on their experience in the classroom.

One of the growing challenges to a coherent sixth form is the proliferation of Post-16 qualifications. Having vertically mixed tutor groups, Year 12 and Year 13 pupils together, is one way of counteracting this. However, with both linear and modular courses now available, even the most well-established unit of teachers and taught can feel the sixth form's coherence tested by the growing multiplicity of routes to university entrance. We have recently adopted a linear approach to A level with most pupils taking AS modules in January of Year 13 rather than Year 12, and thus maintaining their commitment to four A levels. With the introduction of the IB Diploma, a linear programme which also emphasises the value of breadth, this will mean that the academic cycle and pace of the sixth form will not be dissimilar, whichever route our pupils choose.

You will naturally be keen to see your pupils take a leading role in the life of the school as a whole, and not simply generating a vibrant sixth form behind closed doors. Opportunities abound in the election of prefects, members of the sixth-form council, charity boards, and peer counsellors as well as senior roles in clubs, societies and representative school teams. A sixth-form centre run by the sixth form itself is a noble goal, if at times a challenging one. Do not be afraid to let your sixth form find its voice metaphorically; its members almost certainly will do it literally in the inevitable sixth-form talent show.

A lucid and well organised approach to university admissions is another hallmark of a successful sixth form. Experience indicates that there is significant advantage in developing a culture of early submission of your pupils' university application forms. Universities appreciate the early expression of interest, even if they operate a gathered field, and the early appearance of offers for university places will have a motivating impact on the year group as a whole.

Heads of department will be able to support the work of sixth-form tutors as mentors throughout this process, but you may like to consider in addition identifying specialist subject advisers whose responsibility it is to ensure up-to-date knowledge and understanding of those course areas or career choices which do not feature in your core curriculum. Medicine and law, for example, will need specialist support from an early stage, as well as recruiting your alumni and parent body in providing practice interviews, work experience and e-mentoring.

But be sensitive about the perception that you or your team do not value as highly those courses and careers which are no less aspirational but perhaps less competitive at university entry. Be active in gathering relevant contextual information to support your pupils' applications for university places. Parents will appreciate the opportunity to explain whether their son or daughter is the first in the family to attend university, for example, or if there are financial or pastoral situations which university admissions officers should be alerted to.

And so, after two breathless years, you bring your cohort of 16 year-olds to the cusp of adulthood and life beyond your sixth form.

As head of English becoming head of sixth form at Portsmouth Grammar School, I was more than aware that the city has a history of restless childhoods. Charles Dickens, the inventor of the Victorian notion of childhood, was baptised in the same city font as I K Brunel, before his family was forced to move on because of debt. Rudyard Kipling was sent from Bombay to Southsea as a boy and had a forlorn time in the aptly named Lorne Lodge. Poet and novelist George Meredith denied he had even been born here. Later he would model for Henry Wallis' famous portrait of the death of Thomas Chatterton, that Romantic symbol of lost innocence.

We hope, of course, that the experience of childhood here today is a far happier one and more uplifting. As head of sixth form you have the enormous privilege of running a major section of the school and of working alongside young people at one of the most exciting stages of their development. And if your pupils are restless to move on by the time they have completed their time with you, you will have done your job well.

The end of your pupils' time in the sixth form is an important rite of passage to mark well: a chance to celebrate their achievements and to commission them in their future lives. The child will indeed have grown into an adult and it is time for you to look forward to hearing what it is they actually end up doing when they reach the age of 25.

Chapter 13

Pastoral plus: the role of the chaplain

Nicholas Seward

'What are we doing?' was the title of a conference for chaplains that I was invited to attend in my first term in the job. It seemed to sum up well a sense that we were perceived as something of an anachronism in many quarters, as was daily chapel. There was a general feeling that chaplains were ephemeral creatures, with a fairly undefined remit, but if nothing else, an important plank in the pastoral structure. I did, however, enjoy six wonderful years in the role before becoming a Head, and what follows will inevitably be a highly personal view of why (and where) I think the chaplain is important, coloured by my own convictions and relatively short experience.

Fundamentally, a chaplain's role is to teach, live, and defend the Christian Gospel, quite apart from any considerations about where he or she figures in the pastoral structure. That statement raises, of course, the wider issue of the foundations of our schools; what they are about now, and how they see the issue of faith(s) in education.

I came to Magdalen College School fresh from a curacy in the Church of England, and enthusiastic about education in a Christian context. Magdalen is an academic boys' day school (although now taking girls too at 16+), with a Christian foundation and daily chapel services. I grew increasingly convinced that an environment which was firm in its convictions could be, perhaps paradoxically, the most tolerant of places in the best sense – not governed by a shallow political correctness, but a setting where real disagreement and debate could take place in an atmosphere of courtesy and respect.

For many pupils, chapel was an important and valuable part of school life, and it was heartening to see this reflected so strongly in the school's ISI report. I was also quite aware that a great many pupils came to chapel with no convictions, or with strongly anti-religious ones. If nothing else, I felt that chapel offered them a chance to learn good manners, and respect for a tradition they didn't share. Many of them came to value it deeply, even if unconverted.

Magdalen operated a policy of conscientious objection: parents could withdraw children from chapel if they did not want to go, but very few did. At my current school, they don't get the choice, and on the whole I prefer that approach, for reasons of community on which I'll elaborate later in this chapter.

So the million-dollar question for any school is: 'What do we believe?' A chaplain makes sense when there is a clear commitment by the school to a particular faith, and where the school sees faith as essential to its identity and values. If there is clarity there, the chaplain has some hope of knowing what he or she is doing.

However, many of our schools will have begun with religious foundations, but will now feel that they must reflect a pluralistic, multi-faith society – in which case I cannot see the case for a single chaplain as such. Why indeed should one view be privileged above others? (Unless, of course, you are going to appoint chaplains for every faith group – which might stretch the patience and resources of the governors' F&GP committee!)

Where a school does *not* see one single faith as one of its defining aspects, it needs to consider how it will deal with the various religious faiths represented within it, and their importance to pupils. As a primary school pupil in Papua New Guinea, I can remember all of us being split off into a multiplicity of denominations and faiths during RE hour, all with their own representatives coming in to the school from outside.

It included a group for those, like me, who came from non-religious homes. We met in the library and had private reading time. There, I discovered J R R Tolkien (amongst other things), but I can't say the whole arrangement was very satisfactory from the point of view of integration or school cohesion.

It is impossible to talk about the role of the chaplain without raising the wider issues of pluralism and the society we live in. Many in our society, and many schools, have bought into the fallacy that it is possible to be 'ideologically neutral'. There is a prevalent belief that religious commitment is somehow a private, optional extra to a common set of public values which all share, whatever their faith or lack of it. But no sincere religious believer or non-believer of any stripe ultimately sees their 'faith' in that way.

The store of public values in this country has been shaped by Christianity for many centuries, and there are strong reasons as to why those values are important in education. Chief amongst these would be the belief that every human being, and every pupil, is of infinite worth and value. What *are* the foundations on which we build the idea of human dignity? The biblical assertion that we are made in the image of God, male and female, is the Christian resource.

Another conviction, stemming from this, concerns human freedom and moral responsibility. Ultimately we are not determinists. We believe that pupils are more than the sum of their genes, environment, and upbringing, and need to be held accountable for their actions to some degree. Even modern science, it can be argued, has its roots in the intellectual convictions of Theism. Tolkien writes beautifully in alluding to scientists as having: 'A devoted love of the physical world, and a desire to observe and understand it for its own sake and as "other" – as a reality derived from God in the same degree as themselves – not as a material for use or as a power-platform.'

From human freedom and intellectual curiosity comes a real tolerance of differing viewpoints. Especially in a school, young people are (or should be) exercising the curiosity to come to their own conclusions about the big questions of life, and debating them with others. A clear Christian foundation encourages that debate by its very nature.

But what of the charge of indoctrination? We had great fun at Magdalen during my last year, when Richard Dawkins came to the school as one of a series of speakers presenting an alternative view of the world. The lively ferment of debate which he generated, in depicting human beings as 'gene-bearing machines' without ultimate value or purpose, was for me what a good school should encourage and be all about. In the weeks that followed, the school's Secular Society organised a vote on the way into chapel. Boys were given voting slips, and trooped past three boxes, labelled 'God', 'No God', and 'Don't Know'. The numbers divided roughly equally three ways; the boys were surprised to find that God had actually won the popular vote (but not half as surprised as I was).

And chapel itself? We had a short service every morning, which had to be a shade less than 15 minutes. We always had a hymn, a reading from the Bible, and usually a message or meditation from me or a member of staff. Where content was concerned, I felt that good traditional hymns were not only fine worship, but had intrinsic educational value, both musically and theologically. The reading of the Word of God was important from a Christian point of view, even though, of course, many did not share such a high opinion of its origin. I always encouraged them to consider it at least as the most significant and important piece of writing in existence, if only for its literary, historical and philosophical impact, and thus worth being familiar with.

As for the chaplain's message – well, with C S Lewis, I thought much of what I did was *preparatio evangelica*. The Christian Gospel should be preached, but it should be given intellectual credibility, if it is to gain a hearing. Dealing with questions such as the problem of pain, the hypocrisy of the Church, religious conflict, and the question of God's existence were important, especially in an academic environment. The aim was to be provocative (in a good way), challenging, and topical. When I heard that A level philosophy classes usually began with a discussion of the logical soundness (or otherwise) of the chapel address, I felt I must be doing my job!

If nothing else, chapel had enormous value in bringing the whole school community together every morning. The service set the tone for the school day, engendering a sense of order, dignity, and respect in proceedings. That's not to say that a school assembly has to be religious, I suppose, but beware! I remember a hard-bitten old classics teacher coming up to me very early on in my time, and saying, "Well, vicar, you should know that I'm an atheist. But I'm broadly in favour of chapel, because if we didn't have chapel, we'd all have to sit through some ghastly citizenship address."

At particular points of the year the value of chapel was especially evident. The annual Remembrance service, for example, brought a tangible sense that pupils connected with a larger reality than themselves. They sounded the Last Post, sang the anthem, and there was always poignancy in prefects reading the names of the fallen: boys as old as them, or not much older, who had shared similar visions and dreams of futures which never came to be. In one year, we lost a much-loved teacher before his time. How important chapel became then, as a focus for grief and loss, and of a community finding closure and moving on. At other times the emphasis was much more celebratory, with carols by candlelight at Christmas, and the annual Commemoration in the University Church, which marked the end of the school year.

So, in essence, chapel has a fundamental and pivotal role to play in the life of a school, and this must be the primary focus of the chaplain. But beyond this, how does a chaplain fit into the wider pastoral and disciplinary structures? This really depends on the gifts and talents that each one brings to the role. Every chaplain will be unique, and I don't think that they should necessarily be seen as *de facto* counsellors. In my current role I'm very fortunate to have two chaplains – one male, one female – to meet the needs of a coeducational boarding school.

Both are wonderful; both operate in completely different ways according to their strengths. One is most definitely a very skilled counsellor who brings a quiet empathy to her dealings with pupils and staff. The other is more of an all-action figure: someone who has worn various 'hats' in middle and senior management, and is thus not automatically sought out in a counselling capacity. Whatever their individual skills-set, though, I think it is vital for chaplains to be fully involved across the range of school life, rather than a peripheral or part-time figure, if they and their message are to have credibility.

Counselling was very much *not* my gift, and I generally left it to those who were far better qualified than me. Getting alongside pupils, however, meant running sports teams, getting involved in clubs and societies, and being a visible presence everywhere and with everyone, as well as teaching a full timetable, running a department, and operating as a housemaster within the pastoral system. Some chaplains tend towards being disciplinarian, whilst others bring more pastoral gifts. As long as the work of chapel and the Gospel is central, I don't see that there need be a conflict between these two aspects of the role.

Since I moved to a new school and became a Head myself, the value of a chaplain to anyone leading a school has become much more evident to me. Having a colleague who sits somewhat outside the normal structures of the school, and who offers a discreet and listening ear, has been a pillar of strength and support. I cannot imagine what it would be like to be without it.

Both my current chaplains also see part of their job as being quiet fire-fighters: trying to deal with miscommunication or 'Chinese whispers' between the SMT and the common room, and getting alongside staff to engender a positive atmosphere, even in the midst of the pressures of a busy boarding environment during report-writing season. This part of the job represents a delicate balancing act for any chaplain, but if done well, it can be of enormous benefit to overall morale. It calls for people who are not seeking their own agendas, or wanting to be political animals, but who are concerned to give themselves sacrificially as servants of the school, and of the pupils and staff. I'm tremendously grateful to be working with individuals like that, and the school is privileged to have them.

A boarding school does, of course, offer opportunities and scope that can be limited in a purely day setting. Boarding schools are very much more *in loco parentis*, and their pastoral role encompasses the child's life much more comprehensively. This includes all of the negotiations with adolescents (and, indeed, with adolescence itself) which can be much less visible when a pupil is only in school during the working day. Houseparents are the key figures here, but chaplains can add a vital supportive presence, and increase the opportunities available to pupils to find a listening and empathetic ear. Their role allows them to drop in to houses on a regular basis in the evening, touch base with house staff, pick up on issues, and often detect a bigger picture which may call for a response at a school-wide level.

I have found them to be invaluable eyes and ears for the senior team, who of course might elicit a very different response by their own direct intervention. Without divulging confidences, those with pastoral oversight can be made aware by chaplains of the tensions and pressure-points facing stressed pupils, and those about whom the SMT should be concerned, *before* such cases become major problems. At times, they can also mediate in the other direction, at least hinting to pupils when the SMT is dealing with a complex pastoral case, about which the view from the pupils' common room may inevitably be limited or distorted by partial information, limited experience of life, or both.

It is sometimes a very difficult line to tread. There is an expectation of confidentiality which, once lost, can scupper any useful or meaningful pastoral role which the chaplain has: I have known it happen in some schools. On the other hand, chaplains have a duty (like all staff) to love the whole school community, and to highlight issues that need to be raised. It goes without saying that where child protection is concerned, a chaplain is duty-bound to uphold the law, which overrides the sanctity of the confessional. Chaplains, like all staff, need to be trained carefully in this area, never to put themselves in a position where they promise a confidentiality they cannot uphold.

Above all, both staff and pupils need to be aware of what the chaplain offers, and why he or she is there. INSET and induction are good opportunities for chaplains to express the vision and foundation of the school, and their role within it to staff. Where pupils were concerned, I always used the first chapel service of every year to explain exactly why it was that they gathered together every morning for an act of worship, and why that was important, whatever their personal feelings about it might be. It was an opportunity to reassure them that it was perfectly all right not to join in with prayers; not to feel they had to agree with anything I said, nor to pretend to a faith they didn't possess.

One could affirm clearly that the school had convictions, but also that it expected them as young people to wrestle intellectually with the meaning of life; and that pupils had permission to challenge views or doctrines they found perplexing (something which they certainly did!). For many with a shy or uncertain faith, this approach allowed them an environment in which they could be nurtured without fear of a vulgar ridicule – although they could certainly not expect to be cocooned from the interrogation of beliefs and values which we all enjoyed. Guidance on discipleship – whether that took the form of confirmation classes or the Alpha course – could be offered, alongside Christian societies, enquirers' groups, or optional communion services during the week.

I've heard many Heads say that the appointment of a chaplain is the most difficult to get right. It is such a multi-faceted role, requiring a minister who is happy to embrace all the different challenges that being the 'school vicar' involves. It is a very different ministry from that of parish life, for example, and it will suit some and not others. I had some extremely happy and fulfilling years doing the job.

Above all I would end where I began – the school must be clear about what it is and what it stands for. If it is, the school will be more likely to be successful in appointing a chaplain, and the chaplain in fulfilling that role. By now, it will be clear that my own philosophy is a straightforward one: for a Christian, the life, death and resurrection of Jesus change everything. That is either true or it isn't. For those of us whose schools believe it is, it has to be the centre of everything that we do.

Chapter 14

Advising on the next stage: an important pastoral issue

John Gibson and Daniel Cross

One of the most important – but not always fully appreciated – aspects of an effective pastoral system is the way in which it guides pupils over the choices which may fundamentally affect their future lives and careers.

John Gibson is Head of a comparatively small rural school, comprising both day children and boarders up to the age of 16 who have a fairly wide range of abilities. By way of contrast, Daniel Cross is deputy head and formerly head of sixth form in a medium-sized school with a strong academic focus and a growing roll, in which tutorial advice tends to centre on choices of A levels and then university.

John Gibson

Whether you work with children at the top, middle or bottom of the academic pecking order (or with all three types); whether they are young or old (or somewhere in between); whether your school is in the centre of a city or the depths of the countryside, some universal considerations will apply. All children need good educational and career advice. They have an entitlement to it, as much on grounds of human justice as in law. Most of the children whom we teach are fortunate to have at least a degree of choice in the next stage for life's journey, whether it involves transferring to another school or college; to a university or – for a declining proportion these days – straight into the world of work.

The age at which children start to exercise a big influence on decisions which were once left to parents continues to go down. And, as chapter 1 reminds us, there are growing pressures facing parents, children and teenagers to get those choices right. All parties concerned need to be aware of the importance of good qualifications; what the available subject options are; what they might lead on to and, conversely, what future pathways an inappropriate choice might rule out. Finally, whether your pupils are tomorrow's professors, captains of industry or are people likely to be in somewhat less exalted roles, happiness and fulfilment tend to go hand in hand with success – whatever the age of the child.

While the pre-16 age-group generally faces fewer options and timetable complexities than the 16-18s, there are plenty of ways in which schools can help to give children varied opportunities to discover their talents and good advice on how to develop them. One is through bringing into school a good cross-section of parents and local supporters to describe their own careers; it often starts with the policeman and the fireman talking to our youngest children, with more sophisticated careers talks following later on.

Another involves putting on events in which the children themselves take a strong organisational role. It is never too early to start. My own school has often uncovered hidden organisational talents amongst members of Years 4 to 6 as they devise and organise their own stalls and competitive activities at our Christmas bazaar, despite the huge learning curve which this creative and entrepreneurial experience sometimes represents for them. Older children collect and distribute harvest gifts to senior citizens in our local village, developing their administrative skills. It also teaches them the arts of teamwork and adaptability. These are qualities that will hold them in good stead in a world of work which will continue to demand skills which are transferable.

Such skills can be further developed by giving leadership experience to as many senior pupils as possible. We took a decision some years ago to replace the prefect system with the concept of the 'senior year': it allows members of Year 11 not only to develop their gifts but also occasionally to make their mistakes in a low-risk context and then to learn from them. Drama gives some pupils experience of being the centre of attention, but it can also play a hugely valuable role in giving others the backroom experience of stage management or technical help.

Offering a good work experience programme – with good-quality monitoring and follow-up – may help to convince a pupil that s/he really wants to follow a certain career, but it can be equally valuable as a process of elimination: some participants discover that the experience they gained was in something that turned out to be the *last* thing they would wish to do for life; even so, they have gained valuable *experience of the world of work*: not quite the same thing as *work experience* itself, but just as important.

And what is all this discovery and development of talent leading up to, in a three to 16 school? Ideally, to the point at which the level of pastoral trust between staff, pupils and parents is so well-established that the choice of next institution is realistic, and the transfer process to it seamless. This cannot, of course, be taken for granted; all schools will have a proportion of parents who are unrealistic about their child's abilities, or who wish to push them towards institutions which are too competitive or too robust for them.

However, in a comparatively small school, discipline can mostly be light-touch in style (all teenagers want to be perceived as grown-ups nowadays); contact between parents and teachers can be regular and generally relaxed. There are few, if any, places in a small school where a pupil can hide away in terms of academic under-performance; everyone knows everyone else.

All this helps to create a good basis for sound advice about 16+ transfer being given by teachers and being received positively by pupils – even though there may need to be diplomatic and sensitive steering along the way. If we have done our work well, our advice will be listened to, and most of our departing Year 11s will thrive in their new sixth-form surroundings. A few may have to be advised that they will find sixth-form work too demanding.

We are all familiar, too, with less confident pupils who underestimate the difficulty they will face if they are suddenly pitched into a much larger institution, filled with extroverts; it may not have sufficient academic safety nets – for example in monitoring pupils' progress around the first October half term. We have all experienced pupils who are attracted by the glitz of a well-run open evening but who fail to discover that their subject and activity choices can't be timetabled or clash with each other – and those who long to break away from the structures of what they perceive as excessive rules and rigid uniform standards, but who in reality need as much structure as possible in their lives.

There is one other group which needs our particular attention. A small proportion of children need to leave a school *before* their 'natural' time – for example, either because of relocation or changed financial circumstances within the family. A good school gives as much advice as it can muster about schools in the area to which a pupil is moving. Within the bounds of sensitivity and confidentiality, it also keeps its staff informed about these unexpected departures and the reasons for them; hard-pressed teachers can occasionally jump to wrong conclusions or even say ill-considered things if (for example) an unexpected letter giving notice of leaving arrives on the first day of term from the parents of one of their tutees. Teaching is a more secure profession than most, and not everyone enjoys our comparative security of employment.

Whatever reason causes children to leave, they should of course be given a good send-off on the final day. Too many children get overlooked when the farewells are being made and the final assembly plaudits being given out, if they happen not to be in the same year group as most of the leavers. Finally, maybe it goes almost without saying that we should never underestimate the distress to a child caught in the middle of an acrimonious family break-up, and that a school should be prepared and able to do almost anything to support a family when one parent dies prematurely.

A school does not earn a strong pastoral reputation overnight: it tends to be built up over years rather than months. But one of the most rewarding things about Headship is the sudden realisation that people remember the kindnesses that you offered many years ago, long after you have forgotten them yourself.

* * * * *

Daniel Cross

At the start of September, as members of Year 11 walk through the school gates, the atmosphere quickly changes. Not only do they appear to be significantly taller, but the focus in assembly and tutorials shifts from study skills and team building to the prospect of making life-changing decisions. These decisions are centred on AS choices, university courses and potential careers. Over the course of a summer holiday pupils are expected to return with a clear vision for the future and we ask them to make careful and thoughtful decisions.

When we consider how long it can take professionals in the adult world to embark upon career changes, I am always impressed by the considerable clarity of thought expressed by pupils of 15 or 16 who have to define their immediate and long term future. They have a remarkable capacity for managing an extremely busy schedule of examinations, sports fixtures, plays and rehearsals whilst happily formulating judgements and plans for the future.

Rarely, if ever, do we hear: "I'm just too busy to think about that right now." On they press, with their social and study commitments, whilst embarking on some of the biggest decisions of their young lives. Supporting the pupils throughout this period are experienced and dedicated teachers. Through the delivery of tutorial evenings and seminars a partnership develops between the school, the pupil and their parents. This creates a knowledgeable community which can help guide pupils through the choices ahead.

One of the first decisions they have to make concerns their choice of subjects to study in the lower sixth. Do they opt for subjects they enjoy, subjects they are good at, or subjects that they have to do as a qualification for the next stage? To ensure that this process is successful, pupils and parents need access to a team of specialist advisors in school. In the past a school might have relied purely upon well-meaning subject teachers supporting the Head and deputy head of sixth form. However, the choices which pupils have to make are becoming ever more complex, for example:

> Chris just doesn't know what he wants to do. He is reasonably good across the board; heading for a top university, but probably not

Oxbridge. He could be a scientist, or he could go on the arts side. He is thinking about the possibility of reading law at university, and knows he will need high grades. He knows that law courses don't have any direct subject requirements. He feels that essay subjects like English and history would prepare him well for law, but equally a scientific combination of physics, chemistry and maths plus one other would leave the science route open if he wanted to go that way.

Sarah feels that she wants to branch out a bit and study something different in Years 12 and 13. After reading the sixth-form prospectus carefully, she would like to study economics, and thinks she would like to study this at university. She also quite likes the idea of politics, which can combine with some economics courses. Oxford has a politics, philosophy and economics course which she likes the look of, so she decides to do philosophy. Psychology is another subject she has not studied before, so she goes for that as her fourth choice.

She has already been reading about her university options and when she does some further research in the careers library and on the internet, she discovers that economics contains quite a lot of maths, and that if you want to read it at university, you really should be doing A level maths. She is not sure about the joint courses but thinks she might want to do economics at university. So she decides that one of her trio of politics, philosophy and psychology choices has to go. But which one?

Given the range of choice, establishing a high-quality UCAS team is essential in delivering a first-class service. In my school the team has grown from a Head and deputy head of sixth form handling the bulk of the applications process to a dedicated UCAS team consisting of six members of staff. This team consists of:

A Director of Qualifications and Progression.

A full time UCAS, exams and careers administrator.

A universities and Oxbridge advisor for science subjects.

A universities and Oxbridge advisor for arts subjects.

A medical admissions advisor.

A nominated member from each department acting as a subject advisor.

One university course that requires specialist advice is medicine. As with many subjects the number of pupils applying to study medicine has increased and the competition for places is extremely high. This is where a specialist medical admissions advisor is invaluable. In my school a science teacher was encouraged to develop this position and soon convinced me of its importance for medical applications. The teacher has developed a weekly 'medical forum', supported by opportunities to listen to leaders in medical research and practice at a local regional hospital.

A significant number of sessions are focused on preparing pupils for interviews and admissions tests. Involving an economics teacher and history teacher to improve the pupils' essay techniques resulted in improved results on the essay section of the admissions test. This teacher focus on style and coherence appears to have made a significant difference in the pupils' performance which leads to a greater number of offers. The medical admissions advisor has become a vital part of the UCAS team and the contribution made to the admissions process is certainly appreciated by the pupils and their parents.

Building a specialist team is an important step in enhancing the service we offer pupils, but the ultimate responsibility for preparing and completing an application lies with pupils themselves. When do you start and how do you motivate the pupils to meet the deadlines? There are no straightforward answers, but in my experience the earlier the process begins, the greater chance you have of success. The lower sixth can be a year of increased freedom and independence from home but there is no doubt that successful performance at AS is vital in improving the offers received from universities. Many pupils are, of course, highly self-motivated to succeed, but some require careful monitoring and a little convincing. This is where the traditional sixth-form team of a head of sixth form and the deputies should be focusing their attention, rather than trying to manage the UCAS process as well. The wide range of social, family and behavioural concerns that arrive on a seemingly daily basis provides the pastoral team with a significant challenge. This challenge should not be diluted by the complex world of university admissions.

One innovative resource which is available to schools but perhaps under-used is its own historic evidence on university admissions. By creating a database of all the successful and unsuccessful applications a school can provide its parents and pupils with a contextually relevant comparison with previous years. It also helps to dispel the urban myths surrounding certain courses and universities and gives a clear picture of the level required for success.

Managing expectations is one of the hardest discussions that pastoral and UCAS staff will have with pupils and parents. This is where a database is extremely useful in guiding appropriate choices. The database can be analysed by subject or university, and it should cover the last five years of admissions data for the school. For each pupil the database can anonymously include the number of GCSEs achieved at A*, A and B, his or her AS results and the decisions of the various universities to which that pupil applied. This unique resource helps to enhance the pupils' knowledge and to improve their decision-making.

However, securing an offer is only one stage in the process and our role should only be complete when we have assisted those who need our support in the days and weeks following the publication of results in August. Results day is an emotional experience for the whole school community, as it draws a passage of time (indeed, a whole stage of life) to a close and launches aspiring young adults towards a gap-year or university.

For the majority, offers are met and plans can proceed with speed. However, there are those who still require our help and a school has a duty to look after those in need. An efficient UCAS team will quickly establish which pupils need our assistance through the clearing process. Usually pupils need to take responsibility for phoning a university, but teachers can offer much appreciated support to parents and relatives who wait anxiously on the fringes. Supporting the pupils should continue over the following weeks as situations change. Parents are extremely appreciative of a phone call which helps to leave a lasting and favourable impression of the school's commitment to their son or daughter's pastoral care.

With a greater number of pupils applying post-A level, the school has a responsibility to ensure that they too remain eligible to tap into the advice service offered by the school. Post-A level applicants deserve the same level of advice and support and the school should embrace them as if they were still part of the sixth form. In doing so the school cements a lasting relationship with its leavers. Indeed, Heads and others will tell you that one of the less obvious aspects of their work (or even their post-retirement activity) can occasionally be giving advice to former pupils three, five, even ten years after they took their A levels. An increasing number of our pupils will end up in jobs far removed from the courses which they chose to pursue at 18, as flexible knowledge transfer becomes more and more important.

Independent schools have the opportunity to offer bespoke university admissions advice tailored to the needs of the pupils and parents. I believe it is essential to develop a specialist team to manage the demands of an ever complex process and parents rightly expect a high quality service. By providing a Rolls Royce service the school fulfils its commitment to the pupils at the end of a long school career. Pupils will remember the care and attention they received when making these life changing decisions and this helps to create a stronger and more cohesive school community.

Chapter 15

Caring for international boarders

Christopher Greenfield

"As boarding staff, we might be guilty of being a little complacent sometimes when it comes to meeting the needs of international students. After all, they have come to the United Kingdom because they believe that our educational system is one of the best in the world. Surely it is up to them to adapt to our methods and not the other way around, right?"

Cheryl Broughton, Housemistress, 2005

British boarding education is now a global resource. For most of the world the UK is the number one choice for those seeking a boarding education in the west for their children. The figures for enrolment of non-British children in boarding schools show a steady rise both in the total numbers and the proportion of boarders in British schools who are from non-British backgrounds.

The 2008/9 Independent Schools Council census data indicated that 21,535 international boarding students, almost one in three of the boarders in schools in England and Wales, were from a non-British background. This had advanced from 2003 when Hobson's report on trends in British boarding showed that 25% of boarders were from overseas.

Of course, there have been international students in British boarding schools since the 19th century. But what was once an exceptional presence has now become a common feature of boarding schools. Put most simply, international students are now vital for the continued success – and in many cases, the continued survival – of British boarding. If we embrace and nurture the global connections of British education, boarding could continue to give the UK a significant niche in the world, despite our demise as a super-power and the seemingly inexorable slide into geo-political insignificance.

But will we grasp this opportunity? Amazingly there are still some schools that seem to be almost ashamed that they have to enrol non-British students. Instead of realising that the enrolment of children from wealthy international families must make boarding education an even more attractive option for British parents in our increasingly integrated global economy, schools openly limit the numbers of non-British students and proudly claim that they have no more than 5% or 10% of international students.

Perhaps this has some appeal for both British and (paradoxically) non-British parents, but what message does this send about a school's attitude to non-British boarders? At the very least it is not a helpful step towards ensuring that boarding schools have a future as much more international institutions. Emphasising the all-round international atmosphere that most boarding schools now have easily marks out a very important advantage that independent boarding schools have over even the very best state schools.

How are schools responding to a possible key role in global education, and the prospect of a redefined but more secure future, whatever is in store for the British economy? One of the first things that the first chief inspector of the newly-established Independent Schools Inspectorate, Tony Hubbard, wrote warned independent schools that they were not all meeting the needs of minority groups 'such as pupils from overseas'.

Others have also warned of complacency among boarding schools about recruitment of international students. An article in *Boarding School* magazine expressed anxiety that the boarding sector might be taking its 'overseas students rather for granted'.

In the ten years that have passed since Tony Hubbard's warning, most schools have moved to a better understanding of the fact that international students are not simply the same as children from the UK except that they don't understand English as easily. But some schools still seem to place most of their faith in meeting their international students' needs purely in the hands of the EFL department. That is what we naively believed 15 or

20 years ago. Now we know better. We have a greater awareness that the social and psychological impacts of crossing cultural frontiers go well beyond linguistic needs, important though they are.

However, anecdotal evidence suggests that at least some boarding schools may be still too complacent about their international recruitment – in other words, assuming that overseas recruits will always be available, no matter how well or badly we respond to their individual and collective needs.

The reaction of boarding schools to the 2008/9 economic disasters was revealing, if what was reported by the newspapers is to be believed. It was widely reported that boarding schools were aiming to keep their boarding houses full by recruiting more international students – but only if they could not fill them with British boarders. So was the international market seen by at least some schools as an emergency reserve supply of boarders, always available if home demand falters?

Seeing international recruitment as a stop-gap measure, as a filler for boarding rolls, cannot be a satisfactory attitude with which to go into this market. Indeed, such motivations might damage international recruitment in the long term. The only socially responsible reason for going into the international market is that the school concerned actively wishes to offer the full benefit of boarding to non-British students. In other words that the school has carefully considered the impact of international recruitment and has, through staff recruitment, staff development, and other preparations, good grounds for optimism that the needs of international students can be met as adequately as those of their UK counterparts.

If international students are enrolled only to ensure that the school budget will balance, it is likely that their particular needs will be wilfully discounted. Why? Because if international students are seen only as a boost to the school income, there is likely to be a strong disincentive on the part of the school administration to admit that additional resources may need to be devoted to these students, to ensure they are given every assistance in maximising their chances of success at the school and in the British educational system more generally.

In my opinion there are two very important reasons why British boarding schools need to give careful thought about the different needs of overseas students, and be ready to dedicate adequate resources to meeting those needs.

First, there is the traditional child-centred approach of British independent education. We do not simply accept at our schools any child whose parents can pay the fees. We consider each child's needs, and only offer a place if we feel confident that these needs can be met adequately through the facilities, staffing and procedures that exist at our school. We rightly agonise over whether it would be right to accept a child with recognised special educational or social needs into our schools; we must be ruthlessly honest in looking at the recognised needs of international students, and accept these students only if we are confident that our schools are equipped to allow them to flourish.

Secondly, there is the more prosaic fact that international parents have a choice. There is no rule saying they must come to the UK for boarding education. The international market place is crowded with energetic competitors who want our share of the market. Unless we can continually demonstrate that our schools are capable of doing a first-class job with our international students, the next generation of international boarders will go to the USA, or Australia, or any one of a dozen other countries that describe themselves as English-speaking.

What is needed from each school is a whole-team approach. What are the 'special' needs that international students bring to boarding schools? A useful check list is provided in the chapter by Hardaker in the 2001 BSA publication *Good Practice in Boarding Schools*. This book is probably on the bookshelves of most boarding school Heads.

The list is expanded and dealt with in more depth in another BSA book, *World Class*. Is this book also on the shelves of most boarding Heads? With all due humility, I believe it should be in staff common rooms and on the desks of all heads of boarding houses in schools which offer places to international students. It is the only published text which takes a comprehensive look at all aspects of the needs of international students in British boarding schools, built on more than 25 years' experience of the International College in Sherborne (which only recruits students from overseas). As such it offers a working manual to any school that wishes to consider whether the job it does with international students is adequate, good or excellent. It also recommends steps to be taken if a school should feel that it needs to do more.

To give a flavour of the needs that are discussed, the list includes:

Pastoral needs such as:

Medical and other information; arrival shock; home-sickness and language; induction, monitoring and management; contributions from international students.

Spiritual needs such as:

How are international students different? Religious stereotypes; personal support; demonstrating respect.

It also examines the vitally important aspect of academic needs, including:

General difficulties; in the classroom; language; attitudes of teachers; classroom management; checking understanding; text books and work-sheets; coursework and plagiarism.

Communications present particular difficulties for schools with international students. As well as possible difficulties directly with the student him- or herself, there are probable wider issues in communications with:

- Parents, agents and guardians, each of whom deserves careful consideration.
- Medical, bursarial and administrative communications also present difficulties.

Staff development needs are also discussed, as they are the key to offering a better experience to international students. The roles of school leaders and school management are naturally very important.

Some of these issues have subsequent sub-headings in which a dozen or more specific aspects are discussed. But the individual needs described in *World Class* are in two broad categories. One is lack of knowledge – on the part of the school as well as foreign students and their parents – and the other is cultural.

The lack of knowledge is not as easy as it might first seem. To quote the former US Secretary for Defense, Donald Rumsfeld: "There are known unknowns and there are unknown unknowns." The known unknowns would include the usual educational data – age, ability, interests *etc* – from the school's side, and fees, arrival date, departure date *etc* from the parents' side.

But the unknown unknowns might include learning styles and previous educational experiences of the new student, from the school's point of view. On the parents' side their unknown unknowns would equally include learning and teaching styles, but also the way in which British education is organised so that, for example, students are placed in year of study according to age, not ability. Why should they be aware that GCSE examinations are usually taken at the age of 16? Or what 'GCSE' actually means, or what 'secondary education' is in a British context?

Unless parents have been educated in England themselves, they may well assume that education is 'done' in the same way in the UK as in their own countries. However, pedagogy varies hugely around the world. Sometimes students arrive in an English boarding school having already had two thirds of their lives in schools in which, for example, students must memorise the text book (generally the case in Islamic countries) or learn exactly what the teacher says, without question or discussion (as in most Far Eastern countries). The inclusion of sport or PSHE on the timetable (especially topics like sex education) may be seen not only as a waste of time, but also as disturbingly anti-educational.

The reluctance of some Far Easterners to participate in, or contribute to, class discussions or group work may not only be because they feel uncomfortable doing so, but also because it is not 'education' to them. Why does the teacher want to know what *they* think? What the student probably wants to know is the right answer – and the teacher is the only one in the classroom who can give that information.

The second category can be grouped together as cultural. We have all experienced culture shocks of sorts: moving to a new locality or a new job (especially in a boarding school) requires personal adjustments to be made in order to cope with changed norms. All children have a dramatic shift in their lives when they start boarding school – even British children.

The upheaval faced by most international students, especially those not fluent in English, is hugely more disruptive. Although many will have a superficial sophistication – they have travelled the world for example, or have a smattering of conversational English – nothing will have prepared them to make the adjustments demanded by a literally alien environment, with different cultural norms, in which everything is conducted unremittingly in a foreign tongue.

Possibly those of us who have worked overseas can glimpse some of the pressures. Those who, in their youth, went on an exchange programme to France, for example, may have a better understanding of the inescapable, perpetual and exhausting effort to try to gather what is going on, to fit in with expectations of good manners, of correct etiquette, and of trying to express one's wishes correctly and without offence, to those who want to look after you, and in a language full of subtleties and pitfalls.

The effects of culture shock may take a week or two fully to kick in. Up until then everything may be new and exciting, different and interesting for the student. Sooner or later, however, home will be missed. The treatment of international and UK students may be quite similar to start with – just keep them busy. After a short while, however, most UK students will have sorted out their friends and will begin to resent being over-organised. International students, however, may still be working out how best to communicate, and may need co-operative activities to extend over a longer time before they too have established friendships. For these students, free time during this period will be when they start to miss their families and friends from 'home'. Homesickness will begin to take its toll.

Dividing the boarding school experience into pastoral and academic, or anything else, may be rather pedantic when looking at the effect of culture shock. For the child on the receiving end, it is all part of one integrated bewildering and exhausting experience. The problem of cultural adjustment may actually be hidden from the host school because of language difficulties, or because the impact of culture shock may manifest itself as a rejection of, or a challenge to, the values of the school – easily seen by the school authorities simply as being naughty or contrary. Punishment will often merely compound the problem, leading to more discomfort for all concerned.

Our personal cultural values are often held completely unconsciously. What we know as right and wrong behaviour has often been absorbed in early life so that we assume that not only are our values universal and natural to the entire human species, but they are also the right values. Thus even when new modes of behaviour have been learnt, an international student may still feel uncomfortable, because deep down he or she 'knows' this is not the right way to behave.

To give two examples: in China it is rude to address a teacher by name. It is polite to address a teacher as 'teacher', or by a similar honourable form of address. For UK teachers to insist on being called by name, face to face, will feel disrespectful, or even rude, to many Chinese students.

Secondly, Thai students know that it is respectful to look at the ground when a teacher speaks to them especially if being rebuked. To insist, as many teachers would, that the student must "look at me while I am speaking at you", will feel to some Thais that they are being made to act in an insulting fashion. Smiling with embarrassment (a common reaction) will not help the student either!

British schools must also remember that encounters with international students are interactive. We expect them to change; but they will also change the 'British' school. Optimally this will be because schools have made conscious decisions to do things in different ways to accommodate and ease matters for international students; at worst it will be because things happen that were not anticipated – because they were not considered ahead of time.

From more than 20 years ago I remember a fight breaking out between a Thai student and an English boy. The Thai tried to explain that he had started the fight because the English boy had touched his head. I put this down to the Thai boy having a lethal temper: I know now that in the Thai cultural tradition the head must not be touched. The English boy had known this and had tormented the Thai beyond endurance. I may have expelled the wrong boy because I did not know all the facts, and concluded that the less articulate boy was in the wrong.

What can be done to reduce the impact of culture shock? One of the first things that can be done is to give some thought to what non-British students who have not had an English educational background might not expect or understand. This requires those involved in every aspect of the school's work to look at what they do with fresh eyes.

For example, in the school prospectus, does the school assume that readers already understand the British educational systems? Do parents overseas already have a working knowledge of the English, Scottish, Welsh or Irish school systems, plus a familiarity with the jargon of schools, especially independent schools, (Michaelmas term, exeats, prefects *etc*), the structure of the school year, know the Christian calendar (Christmas and Easter holidays), and the ages associated with each year group and each examination, so that they can understand what the prospectus says?

The International College's prospectus is the only one I am aware of that has been written completely with overseas parents in mind. It is the product of decades of experience at the College, and we are still making improvements. (Copies can be downloaded from the International College website: www.sherborne-ic.net)

But this is only one aspect. What will students themselves expect in class, and in the house? What about food? Are sport and chapel compulsory? Getting all staff to think about what will be strange, and perhaps surprising, is the first step towards trying to prepare non-British students to adjust their expectations for their arrival. Home students may also benefit from this work, especially those starting boarding for the first time.

What about the language barrier: how can that be overcome? Obviously translating key information is valuable, but what about encouraging your representatives overseas (agents) to visit you? If they are helping students apply for your school, it would be a good investment to get them to your school when they next visit the UK, and for you to take their visit even more seriously than parental visits. If we roll out the red carpet for parents, we should uncork the champagne for agents!

Whereas parents are paying the fees for one, or two, children, and may help persuade one or two other parents to consider your school, agents are doing this all day, every day of the year. It is the way they earn their living! If they can not only guide parents to you, but start the process of helping parents understand what your school and the systems and processes of English education are really like, they will be helping everyone.

Every school has a choice about whether to offer a place to a non-British student or not. Deciding to offer a place to, and accept, a non-British student therefore comes with a moral imperative that the school will do all it can to ensure that this student, as with all students, will succeed. This cannot just be left to the house staff or to the EFL department. It requires a team effort from every part of the school with the implication that there should also be a team leader.

The biggest single step any Head can take towards helping prepare his or her school to do the best it can for non-British students is to create a senior position as the head of international students, or the co-ordinator for international students. This should have SLG or SMT status since the post-holder will have to offer advice on whole-school issues, as well as take an active part in helping academics, house-staff, sports staff, marketing and registry staff, medical staff and administrative staff, to take the necessary steps to prepare for working with international students.

The position will need the wholehearted support of the Head, since there may be some staff who could be resistant even to considering any possible changes: "I treat them all exactly the same, and it doesn't seem to have harmed anybody." Perhaps not, but that's not the same as doing our best for everybody.

If this chapter has struck a chord with any Heads who now might be wishing to improve, or simply review arrangements at their schools for international students, there are several steps that could be taken.

1. Select some of the literature from the 'further reading' list which follows and take action based on it.

2. Scan the BSA staff development programme, and ensure you or a senior colleague attends any sessions focused on international students.

3. Join and support the work of the Association for the Education and

Guardianship of International Students (AEGIS) and also benefit from their seminars and conferences.

4. Join the British Council to support its new-found enthusiasm for promoting boarding schools overseas, and take advantage of relevant conferences, workshops, seminars and exhibitions that they organise.

5. Ask BSA to arrange for someone to visit your school either to offer advice on possible improvements, or to hold an in-house staff development session for all staff or for particular sections of staff to start them re-examining how the work that they do could be made more accessible, comprehensible and helpful to international students.

Further Reading
Good Practice in Boarding Schools (Holgate, BSA, 2001)
World Class - meeting the needs of international students in British schools (Greenfield and Hardaker, BSA, 2005)
Working with International Students - a training manual (Lago and Barty, UKOSA, 2003)
International Students under 18 - guidance and good practice (UK Council for International Student Affairs (UKCISA), 2008)
Bridging our World (Barty and Lago, UKCISA, undated)
Planning and running orientation programmes for international students (Green and Healy, UKCISA, 2008)
Learning to think Korean (Kohls, Intercultural Press, 2001)

Two short documents produced at the International College may also be of interest (copies may be obtained, at cost, from: reception@sherborne-ic.net):
Previous educational experiences of International College students (2006)
Chinese pupils and their learning preferences (2009 - a précis of a 2001 article by Woodrow and Sham)

Chapter 16

Pastoral issues in a world of global communication

Karl Hopwood

When we consider some of the complex issues around the ways in which children and young people use the internet and perhaps more importantly the risks that they face, it is vital that we have a true picture of what they are *really* doing on-line, as opposed to what we and their parents might like to think they are doing on-line.

The internet can provide adults with a window into the lives of children and young people in a way that was never there in the past. Children have always grumbled about their parents and teachers, but when they do this on-line, the targets of their unhappiness can sometimes see what is being said.

Many adults think that the best way to protect children and young people from the possible dangers of the internet is to simply prevent them from accessing the areas that might put them at greatest risk. This is clearly not the way forward. Children and young people will find a way to navigate around the barriers and filters that are put in place and will indeed manage to access the materials that their parents and teachers are trying to prevent them from seeing. As the old saying goes: "There are three ways to get something done: do it yourself; hire someone to do it; forbid your children from doing it!"

Children and young people need to be partners in their on-line safety: it should not be something which is simply done to them, as this will drive their activity underground. Take for example the ten year-old girl who explained that she has two Bebo profiles. When naively asked why, she replied that she has the real one that she uses on a daily basis, and then the one that she shows her parents...

Clearly, the internet can be seen as either good or bad. There are those who think it is the greatest thing ever invented; it has changed the way that many of us live our lives; it provides wonderful opportunities for everyone and has revolutionised the way that children and young people learn. On the other hand, some think that the internet has taken away our freedoms; it exposes our children to huge risks and they must be protected from it at all costs before it destroys their childhood.

Whichever view one holds, the internet is an incredibly powerful tool. It has provided amazing opportunities for all who use it, but in many ways it reflects real life. In the 'real world' there are many good and well-meaning people, but unfortunately a smaller number of individuals who do not have our best interests at heart. The internet is the same: it cannot be seen as good or bad as a technology or a tool. However, the people who use it can of course be good or bad.

A crucial message that we have to get out to children and young people is that the internet mirrors the real world and as such contains risks. There are a number of difficulties that we encounter when we talk to children and young people about their online behaviours and experiences.

First, they tend to use the internet in places that they think are safe, such as school and home. As parents, carers and educators we are keen for children to feel safe in these places for very good reasons: we know that children will learn and thrive in an environment in which they feel safe. However this means that they then tend to use the internet with a false sense of security, thinking that nothing can go wrong when they are at home as this is a place traditionally seen by most children as safe. This is clearly illustrated by the comments of some young people: "How can we come to any harm when we are sitting at home? Nothing really bad can happen..."[1]

Children say and do all sorts of things on-line that they admit they would never do in the real world, and we need to ask why. In addition to this false sense of security about home and school, we also know that the neocortex has not developed in the brains of children and adolescents to enable them to appreciate and understand risks. So although there are many things that we as adults would recognise as risky or even dangerous, children and young people are simply not equipped to deal with or understand those elements of risk.

And not only that. Although children and young people can very often demonstrate their expertise at some of the more technical aspects of the internet and associated tools, they do not yet have the life skills to be able to best protect themselves – and more importantly to recognise risk. Adults (or most of them, at least!) of course do have these skills: they have developed worldly wisdom and a lack of naivety; they tend to be experts at keeping children safe in the off-line world.

As Tanya Byron explained in her research into harmful content on the internet, there are a number of risks. The Byron review categorises these risks into what is now commonly referred to as the three Cs, content, contact and conduct. At first sight the table of risks (overleaf) can seem overwhelming and can often scare parents, carers and teachers to the point of denial: how can they possibly address all of these things, especially when they don't understand the new language of the internet, what peer-to-peer software is, why apps are so important and why everyone is twittering?

It is very easy for adults – who are often referred to as the digital immigrants, with their children as the digital natives – to become very wary of anything to do with the on-line world and to feel that they are indeed powerless to be able to do anything to help to protect their children. Yet if we consider for a moment the risks to children and young people left to wander around any of our cities after dark, we would come up with a similar list of risks. None of this is new: it is simply that the internet provides a new mechanism or medium for children to access some of these things.

Take the risk 'exposure to pornographic material'. This is a risk that has been present for a long time. Children will have seen pornography on the shelves of their local newsagents, although admittedly this would once have been more difficult to access than it is nowadays with the internet. A 14 year-old boy wanting to access some adult pornography before the arrival of the internet would have had to either know someone who could provide this, or take the risk of buying it himself and other people finding

		Content: Child as recipient	Contact: Child as participant	Conduct: Child as actor
Opportunities	Education learning and digital literacy	Educational resources	Contact with others who share one's interests	Self-initiated or collaborative learning
	Participation and civic engagement	Global information	Exchange among interest groups	Concrete forms of civic engagement
	Creativity and self-expression	Diversity of resources	Being invited/inspired to create or participate	User-generated content creation
	Identity and social connection	Advice (personal/health/ sexual *etc*)	Social networking, shared experiences with others	Expression of identity
Risks	Commercial	Advertising, spam, sponsorship	Tracking, harvesting personal information	Gambling, illegal downloads, hacking
	Aggressive	Violent/gruesome/ hateful content	Being bullied, harassed or stalked	Bullying or harassing another
	Sexual	Pornographic/ harmful sexual content	Meeting strangers, being groomed	Creating/uploading pornographic material
	Values	Racist, biased info/ advice (*eg* drugs)	Self-harm, unwelcome persuasion	Providing advice *eg* suicide/ pro-anorexia

out. We all realise how easy it is to access this material with the arrival of the internet.

So, what are children and young people actually doing when they are on-line? They are multi-tasking in a way that we can only dream of. A quick look at the desktop of a teenager demonstrates this: multiple chat conversations; social network profiles; homework; music; perhaps some video content. If we focus on some of these elements we can see how important it is to never make assumptions about young people and the internet.

Most young people today download music from it. The day of the CD, tape or vinyl record has pretty much gone now and people of all ages have moved to using MP3 and MP4 devices. Although most children and young people are downloading, many are not paying for this. Often this is not simply because they have no regard for copyright: rather that they have never been taught about these issues. Intellectual property and plagiarism are complex issues for adults, let alone children.

Take for instance the case of a 14 year-old who was using peer-to-peer file sharing software in order to download films from the internet which had not been released in the UK. He then rented these movies to friends for what he pointed out was quite a reasonable price. He had a menu of choices available and had taken some time and effort to publicise the 'service' that he was offering. When questioned about what he had done, he suggested that most teachers in the school probably had music on their computer that they hadn't paid for. Perhaps he was right!

Another assumption centres on young people and passwords. Two 14 year-old girls had listened to some information about on-line safety and then commented that it was actually a sign of true friendship to share your password with someone else. Although incredible to most adults, these girls pointed out that no one had ever talked to them about the importance of passwords; about creating strong ones; and about the need to protect this information and certainly not share it with anyone. More worryingly perhaps are the adults who admit to using their children's names for a password or those who confess to having lots of passwords, stored in a folder on their computer called 'passwords'...

School is the perfect place to talk to children and young people about some of these issues – it is clear that they will not work these things out for themselves and, making the assumption that they might, is dangerous as it can put them at risk.

Gaming

Gaming is another pastime which is growing in popularity, especially among younger users, but despite parents' assertions that their children are wasting their time playing games, research is now finding that they are actually learning at the same time. As Marc Prensky states: 'Game-playing is as beneficial to children's development as reading.'[2] Moreover, speaking about *World of Warcraft*, Green and Hannon[3] point out that:

> To be an effective World of Warcraft guild master, one needs to be adept at many skills: attracting, evaluating and recruiting new members; creating apprenticeship programmes; orchestrating group strategy; and managing disputes. All of these skills are readily welcomed in the modern workplace, and they are set to become even more valuable.

As with any activity for children and young people, there needs to be an element of balance. It would clearly be inappropriate for them to spend all of their free time playing computer games, but to suggest that children are learning nothing from such activities is wholly inaccurate and only likely to alienate them.

Here is a case study. The parents of two boys, aged nine and ten, came into their school to ask for help. The problem was that the boys were playing on-line games until 1am and were having great difficulty in getting up for school in the morning. The parents were understandably concerned and turned to the school for some assistance. Reading this in the cold light of day, it is easy to suggest that the parents just needed to take control of the situation and parent correctly: presumably they would know exactly how to deal with a child of nine or ten who refused to go to bed at a given time or demanded to be able to stay up and watch a television programme until 1am.

However the problem arises when we talk about an on-line game. Parents and carers are often fazed by the fact that a game is on-line. Very good parents can find themselves at a loss as they are compromised by the 'on-line' part of the game or activity. Essentially, if the same basic principles of good parenting are applied to both on- and off-line situations, it will be possible to achieve a desired outcome. In this particular situation the school was able to provide some support, but another interesting issue is raised here: where does the school's role start and stop in relation to this type of issue? It falls outside the school day: who is responsible? Clearly in this situation the parents need to take charge, but if they feel ill-equipped to do that and come to the school for support, what should the school's response be?

In another situation, a headteacher was greeted by an angry parent one morning demanding to know what was going on in the school as someone in her nine year-old son's class had phoned them at three o' clock in the morning to say: "Quick – is Billy there, the castle's being invaded and I need some help!" The boy making the call was sitting at his computer quite oblivious to the time, it seems, and whilst playing a game with others from all over the world, he suddenly discovered that his castle was being attacked and that he needed his friend's support to defend it. Again, clearly not something that should have been raised with the school and probably more of an issue for Billy's parents, but nonetheless, the issue did arrive at the school and therefore action of some sort was needed.

Sexting

A portmanteau of sex and texting, sexting is the act of sending sexually explicit messages or photos electronically, primarily between mobile phones. This term, first used in the US, refers to the practice of self-generating harmful or inappropriate (and sometimes illegal) content which is then posted on-line or sent to others, often using Bluetooth enabled devices.

Unfortunately this phenomenon is becoming more and more widespread, with many schools talking about teenagers who have engaged in this. This takes us back to our initial comments about young people having a false sense of security when they use the internet. One of the risks that they take is in publishing inappropriate images of themselves posing in a sexually provocative manner, or even naked or performing sexual acts such as masturbation.

Here is another case study. A 13 year-old girl had a slightly older (15) boyfriend and one evening sent him a topless photograph from her computer that she took with a webcam. The girl thought that she was sending this for his eyes only, although it turned out that he had three friends with him at the time that the picture was sent. The girl was at home when she sent the image. The following day, the girl became quickly aware that many people had in fact seen and had a copy of the picture that she had sent. Devastated by this, she went home and confessed all to her mother, who then contacted the school for advice and also demanded to know what they would be doing to the boys who had forwarded the image.

The girl found it very difficult to articulate why she had sent the image in the first place, although she did talk about feeling safe and that she was in her own bedroom with her own things around her. She even talked about the fact that her mum and dad were downstairs, further reinforcing the fact that young people feel safe and almost invincible when they are at home. The girl also commented that she trusted her boyfriend and never believed that he would have shared this image with anyone else.

She pointed out that she would never have done this in the real world and that she didn't have a sexual relationship with him. Further discussion revealed that although she knew that he would be able to see the picture of her half naked, not having to see him looking at it made it easier for the girl.

Probably the one thing that the girl was finding most difficult was the fact that she actually couldn't be sure who had seen the picture and whether all copies of it had been deleted. The probability would be that there were still copies somewhere and that the image could be distributed again at a later date. Totally devastated by this, it is unlikely that the girl will ever fully get over it. She had given absolutely no thought to the possible consequences of what she had done and had never considered the wider implications.

Social networking

This relatively new phenomenon has had its roots in society for a long time. Twenty or 30 years ago, parents and society positively *encouraged* children to network with other young people. They were told to join the local football team, youth club or Scouts and Guides; they were pushed to spend time outside 'networking' with other children and young people (although it wasn't called 'networking' if you were a child, rather than an adult working in the City). The children who were able to take part in an exchange visit with a child from another country were seen as privileged indeed.

The purpose of all of these opportunities was to socialise and mix with others, as this was considered to be a positive experience which would enhance the lives of children and young people. Now, social networking provides an opportunity to network with other like-minded individuals all over the world. No longer is this benefit restricted to the privileged children whose parents can afford to send them on the school trip.

We know that most of our children and young people are using social networking sites – yet we tend to worry about this and view it as a bad thing, because we are concerned about who they might talk to. Did parents in past times know all the members of the youth club or Scouts, or did they rather rely on and trust the judgement and common sense of their children to deal with any issues?

Once again we need to remind ourselves that the best way for parents and carers to keep their children safe on-line is to talk to them. Taking an interest in what they are doing (as opposed to spying on their internet use) will help to build an important dialogue and ensure that children and young people know that they have somewhere to turn to in the event of a problem arising.

Of course children will only tell us the things that they want us to know, but this has always been the case. Pre-internet, good parents would ask the questions: where are you going; who are you going with; who else will be there and what time will you be home? Realistically though, the answers to those questions may not have revealed the whole truth. Parents are usually pretty good at keeping children and young people safe in the real world and indeed take this part of their role very seriously. Now, in the virtual world they need to do the same, asking the same questions and monitoring in the same way.

Meanwhile schools have a vital role to play, both in backing parents up in their efforts, and in advising them about how best to tread this sensitive line between being protective and yet not overbearing.

References
1. Taken from Byron, T., (2008) *Safer Children in a Digital World: The Report of the Byron Review*. London: Department for Children, Schools and Families, and the Department for Culture, Media and Sport (2008). Retrieved from: www.dcsf.gov.uk/byronreview/
2. Prensky, M., *Don't bother me mom – I'm learning*. Paragon House, 2006.
3. Green, H., and Hannon, C., *Their Space: Education for a Digital Generation*. Demos and Grunwald Associates, 2007; and 'Creating and Connecting/Research and Guidelines on Social and Educational Networking', in *Final Report for Becta, KS3 and KS4 Learners' Use of Web 2.0 Technologies In and Out of School*. National School Boards Association.

Chapter 17

Dealing with challenging teenagers

Peter de Voil

Dealing with difficult teenagers is one of the most challenging, but also one of the most stimulating, aspects of teaching. It is natural for some (but not all) teenagers to rebel; to question authority; to act in unpredictable and sometimes unacceptable ways. It is that period of development when adolescents are 'discovering themselves': establishing their identity as teenagers; asking serious questions for the first time; and establishing or renegotiating relationships, most importantly with their peers but also with their parents and teachers. As an American actor once said, "Adolescence is that period in a kid's life when his or her parents become more difficult."

In schools, the timetable is carefully planned and rigidly structured, usually for the benefit of teachers and examination boards. However, teenagers may have a very different mental set of priorities, in which their aims and deadlines are at odds with the expectations and requirements of their teachers. Research has also shown that the brains of teenagers are not fully developed; in particular that part of the brain that controls organisational skills.

Thus the need to plan ahead, to meet deadlines or to devise an effective revision plan, may simply be beyond the ability of some teenagers without help from a sympathetic teacher. The extract by Jonathan Smith at the end of this book gives you an interesting fictional example of this. It is sometimes hard for teachers to understand this, as most of us have been successful at school and have usually enjoyed the experience, as a result of which our patience with the dilatory or negligent student can be limited.

It is worth remembering that parents often find this stage of development in their children very testing. One of my favourite questions came from a teenager: "My parents are having difficulty coping with my adolescence; what can I do to help them?" Parents are bewildered when their delightful and charming child appears to turn into an uncooperative, untidy, uncouth lout. (Remember the quotation from the Eton housemaster in chapter 1?)

At the annual induction day for new students aged 11 or 13 and their parents, I used to warn the parents that this might happen and that, if it did, they should resist the temptation to blame the school and continue listening to, and loving, their child, albeit through gritted teeth! Nevertheless, some parents will expect the school not only to deliver academic success but also to produce a perpetually well-behaved and well-adjusted child. Some will take issue with the school if this does not happen – and will also complain about the behaviour of other people's children and ask what the school is doing about it.

A school has to maintain order and create an effective learning environment. It will expect high standards of behaviour and will have both rules and guidelines. These will include sanctions for those who fail to meet those standards. I have, however, often had to remind teachers that the word 'discipline' means training and not punishment! Of course, students have to learn that actions have consequences, but the aim of all schools must be to train students to acquire self-discipline and to take responsibility for their own actions. Staff meetings at which students' progress is discussed will often hear staff complaining that a student's behaviour is so disruptive in class that the progress of the rest of the class is suffering, or asking why such and such a sanction has not been imposed on a student who has broken a particular rule.

Heads are often in a difficult position; they need to support staff and to show they have not gone soft on discipline. However, schools usually claim to operate an effective system of pastoral care and to treat every student as an individual. Heads will therefore also need to take into consideration the particular situation and circumstances of each individual – some details of which may need to remain confidential.

There is often a tension between the needs of an individual and the school community, but the automatic imposition of formulaic punishments is not always in the best interests of either party.

Some schools discuss students' progress in staff meetings at regular intervals. While this can be good practice, as staff need to be informed about progress or the lack of it, too often attention focuses on the 'bad guys', who then gain a reputation for misbehaviour and become branded as troublemakers. This can then become a self-fulfilling cycle. To avoid this, in my first school as Headmaster, I stopped these meetings and asked small groups of teachers with pastoral responsibility to discuss any students in this category and to come up with recommendations. This resulted in a much more positive outcome.

However, some examples of misbehaviour may be too serious or too intractable for a school to forgive or forget, such as serial theft, physical assault, drug dealing or significant vandalism. I recall a student who broke all the windows in the music school, which was a statement of his anger and a cry for help at being 'rejected' by his mother and stepfather and sent away to a boarding school.

This was not his first serious misdemeanour and I had to ask him to leave, but for a first offence a school should generally allow students to recover from a 'mistake' by giving them a second chance. If a school has to expel a student, I believe we have all failed. Sometimes school rules can be too rigid and can prevent a school from having a flexible approach, but in surveys of what parents want and expect from a school, good discipline is often near the top of the list. Independent schools especially cannot ignore this.

Boarding schools tend to have to deal with more problems of a disciplinary nature, and I know of several Heads or deputies who keep Monday morning free of engagements so that they are available to deal with incidents that have taken place over the weekend, when children were bored or simply had too much free time, or failed to take advantage of the activities being offered.

Here the role of the houseparent is crucial – or the house tutor, if a student does not get on with the houseparent. He or she is extremely influential in a boarding student's life, and it is a difficult role because s/he has to be both a friend and an upholder of discipline – just as a real parent has to be. As a houseparent or tutor, it is important to spend time and effort to get to know the boys or girls in the house really well and to establish a relationship of trust and mutual respect.

If you don't teach a certain group of students but have a pastoral role, it is important to try to get to know them outside the classroom. Students will welcome interest in, and support at, their extracurricular activities (sport, drama, music or debating, for example): it is much appreciated if you are able to congratulate tutees on their performance or achievements outside the classroom. I have sat for many hours with an injured tutee or member of my house in casualty at the hospital, and this has proved invaluable in helping to get to know my tutees better!

If a good relationship can be developed, dealing with crises in their lives becomes much easier and the prospect of a positive outcome is significantly increased. Your tutees will also be more likely to confide in you, or to come to you for advice if they have any problems. Such problems may involve not only disciplinary infractions, but also bullying; troubled relationships or family matters such as divorce; serious illness; or even a death in the family. In a boarding school, the houseparent or tutor is likely to get to know certain students very well – better than anyone else on the staff. There will be occasions when they will want to support a student who is in trouble and recommend leniency, or a second, or even a third chance, because of particular circumstances. Unless it feels that it has absolutely no room for manoeuvre, a wise school will recognise and accept this.

These days it is usually good practice to make early contact with parents if a student seems to be getting into trouble by failing to meet expected standards of academic achievement or behaviour. Making parents aware at an early stage and working with them to identify the problem and work out a solution can often lead to a successful outcome for all concerned.

When students bring problems to you, the issue of confidentiality may arise. To what extent can you promise it? Schools will usually have a policy about this and make it clear that staff may need to share certain confidences. Unless you are a doctor, a counsellor or the school chaplain, your loyalty has to be to the school and your employer, and you cannot keep confidential information that may relate to anything illegal, such as stealing, drugs or under age sexual activity.

In a day school it is more difficult to establish such a relationship. The pastoral system may place considerable responsibility on form tutors, who have many routine duties to perform. It is important that the school provides the time, the training and the support to enable a tutoring system to work properly and effectively. Form tutors may also have 20 or more students to look after and only a short time each day to do all this. And they are unlikely to have time to attend all the sporting fixtures and performances supported by their opposite numbers in a boarding school.

Some teenagers may have a behavioural problem relating to a specific learning difficulty or special educational need. We are familiar with students with dyslexia, for example, and through staff training teachers are much better equipped to understand and address their learning difficulties than was once the case. Parents are usually keen to have their child tested to find a diagnosis, so that s/he qualifies for extra support and extra time in public examinations.

These days such students may be less likely to feel inadequate or inferior but producing accurate work on time is more difficult for them and they may experience frustration and low self-esteem. This can lead to behavioural problems in the classroom, particularly if academic expectations are very high. Such students may be unable, rather than unwilling, to meet expectations, or it is possible that the behaviour of a student with ADHD, for example, may be impulsive or unpredictable. It is likely that a student in this situation will have been identified and diagnosed, so that staff are informed and appropriate methods of support put in place. Finding a teacher prepared to develop a special relationship with such students and to meet them on a regular basis can be extremely helpful and will often be the best way to boost self-esteem and encourage cooperation and compliance.

In some cases, a school may *not* be able to help a student. In such cases, the solution will be to find another school with a reputation for dealing successfully with students with learning difficulties. I remember a student with ADHD who was so frustrated that he would take out his frustrations on the school fabric: the school could only take so many holes in the ceiling before it was agreed with his parents and his psychologist that a different school with a much higher staff-student ratio was needed.

Another student with this condition was escorted back to school by the police for vandalising a car parked in the street. As the car was abandoned and derelict, the boy thought he had done nothing wrong – it was perfectly logical to him. He had not considered any consequences, such as the way it looked to the bystander who reported him or the reputation of the school. Fortunately, the police were not particularly concerned and a conversation with the boy in the presence of his mother seemed to be the best solution, so that he could begin to understand how such behaviour affected others and was unacceptable.

My experience suggests that many cases of bad behaviour are seen in students from dysfunctional families; the resentment, anger or guilt that can result from separated or divorced parents will often manifest itself at school in the form of attention-seeking behaviour or lack of application and achievement in the classroom. When I was a housemaster, one such boy was reported to me for making a large hole in the wall of the dormitory. When questioned, he replied that he had taken out his frustration on the wall because I had told him that under no circumstances was he to hit another boy! As a result, he had to pay for the repair and do an hour's work in the house garden, something he thought was appropriate and fair.

The school cannot always do much about this beyond showing sympathy and understanding, but the support and advice of the school counsellor may help. A boarding school often becomes the repository of such children and it can provide some stability and serve as a safe haven from argument and confrontation at home. I can remember a sixth former thanking me for studying *Who's Afraid of Virginia Woolf?* with his English class, as he said it had helped him understand his parents!

For some students, whose relationship with their parents has broken down or is mostly confrontational, access to a sympathetic teacher, either formally through a designated tutor or informally through another member of staff, can be extremely important. Such a relationship can build up trust and result in a friendship that will often be remembered much later in life. It is important when addressing bad behaviour with a teenager to remember what *not* to do: never to lose one's temper, never to shout and never to humiliate the young person.

The teenager will usually know that s/he has done something wrong and that s/he is in trouble; it is the tutor's role to get the student to acknowledge this and ideally to bring matters to a conclusion that will prevent a repetition of the rule-breaking or inappropriate behaviour. It is also important always to explain carefully what is expected and why, to give the reason behind a rule or requirement. The old-fashioned answer: "Because I say so" simply won't do these days, where teenagers are concerned!

This may involve a punishment or some kind of sanction, but it is part of the recovery process, and it is something that most young people will expect, as they nearly always have a strong sense of justice and fair play. Part of the tutor's conversation with a miscreant must be directed at trying to find out why a particular incident has occurred. The teenager concerned may be in denial, may be defensive, embarrassed or even belligerent – and possibly frightened if the consequences of the offence are serious. Boys and girls will usually protect their friends and may lie about something they have done and deny involvement.

Listening skills are important and as a tutor I have usually tried to talk to a miscreant on my own, as this enables tutor and tutee to have a conversation in which each person can speak freely and perhaps reach an acceptable conclusion, or even make a deal! My technique is to invite a student in trouble to sit down, perhaps offer a cup of coffee, and invite him or her to talk and explain the situation: how and why s/he got into trouble, what the consequences are, why s/he thinks this behaviour is unacceptable, what the consequences might be, and so on.

I have never lost my temper or raised my voice on these occasions, although I have always made clear the seriousness of an offence and my disappointment or displeasure, as appropriate. It is important not to appear confrontational or threatening, but to remain patient and focused and to listen. I once spent nearly an hour with a student in trouble and said very little. He did all the talking, but at the end he thanked me for my support and advice!

Hectoring or lecturing a student is unlikely to be productive: we want to encourage the student to believe that it is better to tell the truth and to give him or her confidence that the matter can be resolved fairly. Teenagers *will* make mistakes and they *do* need to be given a second chance (within reason!) and the opportunity to recover from them. Sometimes I begin an interview by asking the student to give me a mark out of ten to measure how he feels about him or herself. This can be very helpful as it may indicate low self-esteem, chronic depression or relationship problems which have not so far been revealed or identified.

Working with foreign teenagers on residential languages courses in the summer holidays presented a particular challenge: to persuade them to cooperate and conform so that they became fully involved and made significant progress. Such students arrived from a variety of backgrounds and cultures; little was known about them; some were definitely sent away by parents to keep them out of the way; time was short and there were very few sanctions that could be applied.

Even on such short courses, the tutorial system was important. It was possible to discover individual talents and interests and to make sure that students were invited to display or share these talents or be given a particular responsibility: on the football field; organising the end-of-course show; or the course photographer, for example. I even put one particularly difficult and argumentative young man in charge of supervising queues, checking on packed lunches and assembling groups for excursions – he was very pleased. The more fluent students helped the less fluent with their homework. Giving teenagers responsibility and a sense of purpose and involvement may well prevent or reduce difficult behaviour.

Young people are easily influenced by their peers. They often act impulsively and follow the crowd. Thus dealing with younger students in a disciplinary situation can be relatively straightforward: once you get to the bottom of an incident, strong words, an appropriate warning or punishment, often with a letter or a phone call home, may be sufficient.

Dealing with older students can be more difficult, and sorting out a problem may require considerable diplomatic or negotiating skills. Confrontation rarely works, and time and patience are often needed to achieve a satisfactory outcome. It is too easy simply to dish out detentions or other punishments, without investigating the causes or the circumstances, and there are too many teachers who will do this. Many times I have worked out a deal, by stressing that living in a school community involves co-operation and that all communities and institutions have rules for reasons of health and safety and for the welfare of the community as a whole. A parent once told me that dealing with teenagers involves a process of retreating from one negotiating position to another!

The nature of offences changes over time. Schools used to expel students for smoking and drinking, after one or two warnings. This has always struck me as sad, because if they are smokers, they may well have become addicted and a different approach is needed. At my day school in Prague, a letter went home for a smoking offence together with the threat of a final warning – but I allowed myself several final warnings as I was not prepared to ask a student to leave the school midway through his or her IB course for a relatively common offence.

Some would say that this was feeble and that the punishment was not for smoking but for breaking school rules, but I have never subscribed to this view. Some schools fine students caught smoking, and I would be happier with this, just as a parent might withhold pocket money for such an offence, although I have never implemented it myself.

Drug use presents a much greater dilemma. It is likely – look at the statistics – that teenagers will try drugs, usually cannabis or ecstasy to begin with. Drugs are easily accessible and relatively cheap. Obviously a school cannot permit drug-taking during the school day or condone it at other times, but the pros and cons of zero tolerance policies can be the cause of fierce debate. Much depends on the philosophy of the Head (and the governors), the ethos and circumstances of each school, and the details of the individual case.

As a Head I have always followed government guidelines and allowed anyone caught experimenting with drugs to return with a 'final warning' contract and a second chance; I have also encouraged self-disclosure without sanctions. Students and parents appreciate the fairness of this. I can recall asking a sixth former to come and see me after tea and asking him what was wrong, as I had suspected from his woebegone expression and listless body language that all was not well.

After a few minutes he admitted that he was regularly taking a small amount of cannabis. He was purchasing it from a dealer in town once a month as he thought it would help him overcome his homesickness. He admitted that this habit was stopping him eating, sleeping and working properly and that he was losing his friends. His parents were living and working abroad and it was possible to transfer him to an international school in their country, where he flourished and went on to gain a place at a good university – a good example of the success of self-disclosure.

I am aware that my approach, at the liberal end of the spectrum, would not suit all schools or all situations, where a more rigid code of discipline could be both necessary and appropriate. Certainly a new teacher needs to know where s/he stands and may need the support of a clearly defined disciplinary structure to which everybody adheres. In a boarding school, if houseparents have too much discretion, this can cause problems when one houseparent is more lenient or liberal than another. Students quickly realise this and may try to use it to their advantage.

There is a related problem here – and possibly with other offences: what do we do if we hear about a student who has taken drugs at a party outside school during the holiday or at weekends? If the school is told about it, it becomes difficult to ignore, particularly if it is widely known – or if pictures have been posted on the internet. It is possible that this is the tip of the iceberg and it could indicate that the school has a problem and that action needs to be seen to be taken to discourage others. However, on one occasion I suspended a boy who smoked cannabis at a New Year's Eve party and allowed him to return to school having signed a contract. He and his parents protested vigorously that it was outside the jurisdiction of the school – and I don't think they ever forgave me.

Unfortunately, some parents and others expect schools to take action on issues and situations off the school campus and out of school hours over which the school has no jurisdiction. We should all be wary of becoming involved in such situations, but this is not always possible – and our duty of care cannot always stop at the school gate. This problem is more common in boarding schools, and I have lost count of the number of times I have visited shops or supermarkets to complain about their selling cigarettes or alcohol to under age pupils.

Occasionally rebuffed, I have asked if they would prefer me to bring it to the attention of the police. I have dealt with a shoplifting situation and arranged for the pupil concerned to be kept in a police cell for a whole Saturday afternoon, before going to collect him. He received a police caution. This was punishment enough. He later spoke about the incident to the whole school in assembly. His parents were very grateful to the school. On one occasion it was reported to me that four-letter words abusing the school had been carved on seats in a bus shelter in the centre of town. I immediately sent the maintenance department in an unmarked van to sand down the benches and remove the evidence! The culprit was never caught.

Increasingly schools have to deal with offences committed via the mobile phone, blogs and social networking sites on the internet. Bullying and intimidation through anonymous messages and embarrassing photographs are well within the capabilities of most teenagers. Schools will have policies about this but some schools – and parents – are only just beginning to realise the nature and the dangers of these forms of communication.

My first case of this occurred where I had to deal with a boy who posted unpleasant photographs and messages about another boy on his personal blog. Unfortunately the parents of the culprit protested on the grounds that their son's behaviour was outside the school's jurisdiction and the boy had not broken the law. I subsequently amended the school policy to cover such behaviour, on the grounds that it could damage the reputation of the school or cause distress to other students for whom the school has a duty of care.

Accusing someone of a misdemeanour is always a delicate matter. Since the arrival of the Children Acts of 1989 and 2004, young people know they have rights, and accusations without actual proof can backfire on the school. If parents and lawyers are involved, things can become very difficult. It is therefore important to get those involved in an incident to write down what they believe has happened, ideally separately from each other to avoid collusion, to explain the nature of their involvement and culpability. Details of any investigations and interviews should also be recorded and kept on file.

Once, as a Head in Prague, four boys were reported to me for bullying; they had allegedly put a plastic bag over another boy's head to intimidate him during the lunchtime break. Two of us interviewed the victim and the four boys, but we could not decide who was responsible, so we decided to suspend them for a day before seeing them with their parents. This did not meet with parents' approval and I was accused of acting like a communist! It is sad that these days the support of parents cannot be guaranteed; years ago parents would have been more likely to support the school and even add a punishment of their own, but nowadays, unless the evidence is clear and unquestionable, a spirited defence of their child and a denial of his or her involvement are just as likely.

Much of this chapter has centred on the role of the Head, housemaster, tutor and sympathetic teacher. However the contribution of the chaplain, school counsellor and house matron or school nurse should never be underestimated. It is not uncommon for students to confide in the matron or school nurse, and it may be appropriate to consult them when dealing with teenagers.

Most schools can also influence behaviour through PSHE lessons, which, if conducted by an inspired and enthusiastic teacher, can explore some of the issues that teenagers find interesting and want to talk about: relationships, bullying, self-esteem, *etc*. Thus, if stealing, bullying or vandalism occur, teachers can be asked to introduce the topic in these lessons and ask the students to come up with solutions and recommendations.

Dealing with difficult teenagers is not easy and can be both frustrating and time-consuming, and we will sometimes fail. It may simply take time while they grow up – and they usually do!

Chapter 18

Difficult encounters with parents

Nigel Richardson

Dear Richard, or (if you prefer), Dear Emma,

Congratulations on your promotion to boarding housemaster so soon after joining your new school. Your previous day-school experience, deputising for the head of middle school, will stand you in good stead: while the demands of the two posts are very different in some ways (as parts of this chapter will show), they also have a good deal in common – not least in the extent to which your Head will rely on your hard work, patience and good judgement.

Commiserations, though, that Mr and Mrs Deeply-Concerned have been in touch with you already. Your predecessor will be able to brief you about all the turbulent communications over their two daughters, Controversia and Argumentia (both now at university). Their much younger son, Contentious, shows signs of being every bit as challenging and divergent – and I suspect the even younger Disputatious will be much the same when he arrives with you next year from his prep school.

In between bouts of deep angst, however (some justified, some not), the D-Cs support the school in all sorts of ways, and you should try to build bridges with them. A reputation for being friendly and accessible will serve you well in the long run. Remember too that they are first-time buyers, both in terms of boarding and of the independent sector itself: like many, they puzzle and worry over aspects of it which they did not themselves experience in their youth.

You asked what advice I might like to pass on for your dealings with people such as them, and I hope it will be helpful if I deal first with the importance of the initial response and then with the three principal means of getting to grips with the problem: emails, phone calls and face-to-face meetings. All have both pros and cons, depending on circumstance.

In your day-school days, I guess you were accustomed to a situation in which parents mostly made the initial contact with what I'll loosely call 'middle management' via phone or email, and in which meetings were mostly by prior appointment. (Impromptu visits tend, of course, to be made by parents of younger pupils, and to the form tutor.) In boarding schools, the phone/email approach may well be the norm during the week, but you will need to be skilled at dealing with parents who drop in unexpectedly after the mid-week match, or when picking up or returning their child at the weekend.

Let's assume that the D-Cs make their initial contact about Contentious by phone. If you are out, make sure that their call is quickly acknowledged: this can help to lower the immediate temperature. If you need time to think about your tactics, don't be afraid to say – courteously but firmly – that you need time to think about an issue, or that you have something else very pressing which you must deal with first.

Occasionally, if you wish to avoid instant entanglement with them by phoning yourself, or if you need time to think about your tactics, ask a member of the house staff or another appropriate third party to make a holding response, stating that you'll be in touch very shortly. But don't overdo this tactic, lest you get a reputation for being remote and aloof. (This is a situation where day-school staff tend to be better defended, because they can ask the school office to make the call.)

But what if the D-Cs make contact by email? You will have checked your in-box regularly and aimed to acknowledge receipt promptly. The principles are much the same: if necessary promising a considered response later; tell them that you need to do some fact-finding. You don't need to concede anything at this stage. Yet even in a boarding school, emergencies apart, you will also need to draw some careful lines in the sand, making it clear that you prioritise all the demands on you. Yes: our parents are busier, and more stressed. However, they can't always assume that you will respond in full, as soon as they want you to do so, at any hour of the day or night.

As a Head, the more I received brusque email messages, the more I found myself looking at the time at which they were sent. A worrying number of them seemed to be written in the small hours of the night (and I *did* allow for time zone variations). Their behaviour is part of a pattern of radically changed expectations about total availability: any Head who has been in post for more than a dozen years or so can confirm the huge change in demands during school holidays.

At one time (especially in a day school) you could shut down the office a week after term ended, secure in the knowledge that the post would more or less dry up. These days, sudden demands on Boxing Day for duplicate copies of an end of term report, or in the small hours of the second Sunday in August for information on the whereabouts of missing trainers, are far from unknown. But I digress...

Even more occasionally, if you prefer, make the first response via a first-class postcard reply, but do it *that same day*. Your generation will, of course, think I'm hopelessly old-fashioned about snail-mail use, but this personal approach still flatters some people, especially if the card has an amusing photo on the back (I kept some school scenes postcards reproduced from pictures in art galleries). Even a non-committal 'I hope very much that we can sort things out,' response implies that you are taking their concerns seriously.

Once the initial response has been made, you will need to decide which form of follow-up is most likely to achieve a positive and time-effective outcome. Listening, hearing, talking and asserting all have their place in your repertoire, depending on the circumstances. When considering the respective merits of email, a phone call or a meeting, remember that research suggests that when conveying a message, 7% is carried by the words, 38% by the tonality of the voice and 55% by the body language.

Email has huge practical benefits to hard-pressed staff of course, especially in routine matters. You may not be able to control its volume, but you can choose when you deal with it. It is excellent for dealing with overseas parents across time zones. It allows group messages to be sent quickly and easily. Yet it can also be hazardous. Incoming, email gives parents such as the Deeply-Concerneds hugely increased instant access to you although I must admit that their email address, dunpraising@kneejerkresponse.com, is not too encouraging. Outgoing, email encourages us to clear our in-boxes by dishing out hasty, ill-considered responses. There is a temptation to press 'send' in haste.

You've done well to pick up their concern about Contentious promptly. Initially you may not know much about the detail, so you will need to consult others. Think carefully about how widely you copy their message to other colleagues (even with a covering note of your own). Email enables you to keep everyone in the picture; as a housemaster you can no doubt make out a case for informing both the form and personal tutors of young CD-C – and, if the allegation looks serious, the deputy or even the Head. But is it strictly necessary to copy them *all* in at this stage? Will it risk making young Contentious a marked man, or a *cause célèbre* within the common room?

Moreover (I hesitate to ask this question, but most Heads will know *why* I ask it): are you sending copies to everyone in the SMT purely to draw attention to your own level of activity, whilst ignoring the dangers of email overload for others?

There needs to be a clear set of guidelines in any school about the distinction between messages *sent* to people and messages into which they are *copied*. Messages should be *sent* only to those from whom a response or subsequent action is expected – *ie* most messages will be sent to just one person. They should be *copied* to people who are being kept in the information loop, or who might possibly want to add their view, but who should think themselves under no obligation to do so.

You should be careful over confidentiality when forwarding messages. *Reply to all* makes it very easy to send messages to the wrong people, and all too many Heads have had to bail people out of such difficulties. I think of the housemaster in one school who received a parental complaint about maths teaching. He was in a combative mood after a bad day, and he drafted a response to the parent, agreeing that the teacher concerned was, in his opinion, a waste of space. But the phone rang as he rounded off the trenchant prose that had briefly made him feel a lot better. Later, however, he somehow managed to send it to the teacher as well as the parent... I think I also heard a rumour that recently, when sending your school's admissions office a reference on Disputatious, his prep school Head inadvertently forwarded a copy to the D-Cs – and that it contained the sentence: 'He is the youngest of four children. Unfortunately the intelligence ran out before the breeding instinct.'

Think carefully too before sending blind (undisclosed) copies. Do they risk being thought a discourtesy if their existence later becomes known? Use the BCC (blind carbon copy) function if sending a message to a group of people, in order to maintain the privacy of individuals' addresses. When forwarding a message, consider in passing whether or not you should inform the original sender by copying him/her in on your action.

In your considered reply, use a specific subject heading: it saves the recipient's time, and makes later reference-back easier for him and you. Be courteous. Unlike face-to-face communication, emails give no obvious clue to tone of emotion, and a hard-hitting message can't be softened with a smile. Remember that a message or response can look much more challenging to the recipient than the sender may intend, so be diplomatic in your choice of vocabulary/phraseology. Avoid the 'cold-print (or cold-type) syndrome': messages which are interpeted as stiff and hectoring may do you no favours longer-term. Never send an angry message until you have slept on it – and had the opportunity to reconsider it the following day; most messages of this type simply put up barriers – especially with Hector and Grungia D-C. Do not use capital letters – although occasionally a phrase in italics can be used to give emphasis. These stylistic issues apply to letters, too.

Consider whether or not a paper copy of the message should be put on file. Incidentally, remember that while email is a valuable method of keeping a professional dialogue going with both colleagues and pupils, there can be obvious risks if it becomes *too* chatty. Assume that an email message is like a postcard: never confidential. Do your emails pass twin tests: 1) would you be comfortable to read them yourself some time later, and 2) would you be comfortable for anyone else to read them? You never know to whom your message can easily be forwarded. *The Independent* (27 October 2005) put the issue very succinctly: 'Never put in an email

189

something you wouldn't want your boss, your aunt, a lawyer or *The Independent* to see.'

Anyway, you should think carefully about whether that speedy email is really the best form of response. Sure: it gets the resolution of the issue under way, and it will make you feel better, but would this message be better left until it can be conveyed voice to voice, or even face-to-face?

As a means of communication, the telephone is more immediate. It is comparatively personal; it invites discussion and feedback, and if used skilfully it helps to create trust and a developing relationship. On the other hand, the person to whom you are talking cannot see your body language or expression, and impulse calls made on mobiles carry the same risks as the hasty email. Phone calls also carry the potential for the D-Cs (who have a tendency to lobby staff in unison from phones in different rooms of their vast house) to try to press you into concessions, so if you decide to try to resolve a difficult issue by phone, do not make the call until you have decided what you are *not* prepared to concede.

Thus, as a method of resolving areas of disagreement, the phone has its limits and sometimes, however much you may be tempted to avoid one, there is no substitute for a face-to-face meeting.

How do you prepare for such meetings? Put yourself out for the D-Cs (and, indeed, any other parent), by letting them choose the time of their visit – within reason. That way, they are less likely to arrive stressed. If they are punctual, you can emphasise how accommodating you have been. If they are late, you start off on the moral high ground. Even the most difficult parent who turns up late will start off by apologising. Try never to keep them waiting yourself.

Prepare yourself psychologically. There are, of course, a few parents-from-hell, but the vast majority are winnable with the right treatment. Try to get inside the D-Cs' mind-set: there is much truth in the old saying of the American Indians: 'You can never understand a man unless you have walked a mile in his moccasins.' Deep down, many parents crave reassurance – and good advice. They find it hard to admit that they are having difficulties with their teenage children at home – so you may simply be the victim of displaced frustration or of the fear of worse strife to come. School fees have risen far faster than inflation in recent years, so you may be the victim of the fact that *both* parents are over-working and over-stressed, with too little back-up at home.

There is a certain category of parent whose anger levels seem to rise in the very act of crossing the Head's threshold as the memory of a perceived injustice from schooldays long ago suddenly comes flooding back. Even though only some of those feelings may be justified, and although the memory plays tricks, some of these recollections may be very real, and they should be respected.

Remember too that even the most sophisticated and professionally successful parents can be at a complete loss when it comes to dealing with their offspring, which will be a special source of frustration to them. They can also feel unaccustomedly powerless when dealing with schools; a tense meeting can hurt them as well as you. Consider the possibility that something entirely unconnected with school has happened in their lives just a short time before they contacted you, and that you were merely the hapless victim of circumstance: it will make you feel better and (far more often than you think) it will also be the truth. Always be prepared for a torrent of anguish with a quite unexpected root cause…

It may help you to see your meeting with the D-Cs as a tactical challenge. Of the many service-providers about whom they fret, perhaps you can be the one who actually helps to put things right? Avoid displacing your own frustration with their children back on to them, however great the temptation. And remember the old maxim that 'We are all God's creatures' – yes, even young Contentious – sometimes quirky, often troubled, all too prone to make mistakes, but *unique*. That is certainly how they will see their child; keeping this in mind may also enable you to keep your temper if the going gets rough later.

Don't assume that you know their children better than they do (especially if they are experienced parents who have been through it with two older ones). Some parents can be very unrealistic of course, but a lot aren't – and there are areas of their children's lives which we know nothing about, however long we have taught them. By contrast, if they say that their child is co-operation itself at home while you are saying that he's been a real pain at school, be prepared to fall back on an old but useful maxim: teachers and parents both have a partial view because they each see two-thirds of a child; but it isn't always the *same* two-thirds. Agree with them that adolescence can be hell for everyone – but that it does get better, with time. Schools and parents have to work in partnership, even though it's not always easy; we are both trying to serve the interests of their child.

Finally, at the risk of stating the obvious: do as much homework as you can on their child, and talk to as many relevant colleagues as possible – so that you are less likely to be thrown off course at the meeting by reference to a different issue about which you know nothing.

Make sure that the room is prepared; if there is any option to set the furniture more informally than the potentially confrontational across-the-desk mode, take it. Greet them at the main door with a smile; it will give you the chance for some ice-breaking small-talk as you walk down the corridor together – a tactic which one of my colleagues once neatly described as being 'offensively friendly'.

Thank them for coming in to see you. Aim initially to establish an atmosphere of common ground ("Useful for us to compare notes") – but keep it brief, and don't lecture them. Sometimes, but not always, a pre-emptive half-apology ("I'm sorry we have to meet in circumstances like this") or a conciliatory opening ("I guess none of us is greatly going to enjoy this meeting, but let's try to be constructive: I certainly intend to be") can be useful – although if there seems to be the remotest risk of the situation you are dealing with having aspects of legal liability, you need to be wary. If they show signs of wanting to write down every word you say, tell them gently that it's not going to help establish a constructive atmosphere if they do – and don't start compulsive writing-down yourself.

I tend then to say something like: "Why don't you go first, and I'll comment from time to time." This enables them to get their anger, frustration, grievance or sense of injustice out into the open at an early stage. Don't interrupt them too much, but if they say something which you clearly disagree with, put down a marker that it is a point to be returned to later (and make the briefest reminder on a small piece of paper in writing that they can see). Try to inject a little humour at some point – and to find some positive things to say about their child, even if it means straying away from the issue immediately being discussed. You may well find it helpful to remind them (not too didactically) of the difference between established facts and perceptions.

Weigh up whether, with the D-Cs, you are dealing with the type of parent who will only respect you if you show that you won't let them walk all over you. Try to sound confident, even if inwardly at that moment you aren't. Know beforehand the limits of what you will negotiate about – especially in the matter of punishments – although it is sensible not to decide on a single option until you have heard their side of the story.

Don't be afraid to make a qualified concession if you've made some small factual error in a complex set of issues. In the same way that an Oxbridge candidate will get more credit for admitting that he got something wrong two minutes earlier in the interview rather than stubbornly trying to defend an obviously ridiculous position, so you will find that it's better to admit to a small mistake than to try to cover it up.

If the gulf between your two viewpoints is too great to bridge, or if the meeting starts to descend into acrimony despite your best efforts, don't be afraid to suggest that everyone should go away and consider things. Occasionally, a second meeting has other uses too, because after the encouraging initial post-meeting phase, parents such as the D-Cs sometimes seem to regress.

If they start to go completely over the top, insist politely and calmly that you will not be treated like that (and pass the details on to your Head, who should be skilled enough to write the sort of letter which makes a protest on this issue, however justified their original complaint). You can offer to do more investigation – which again will give you the chance to seek advice from further up the school hierarchy before you contact them again. Never lose your temper, even if they do; it is possible to be properly assertive whilst remaining calm and polite. However things end, try to agree on a summary of the point to which the meeting has got them and you – and, if necessary, the issues still needing resolution, and possible ways forward.

If the meeting has even a moderately reasonable outcome, write to them briefly afterwards, either a simple message thanking them for coming in, or a letter which sets out the main headings of agreement and disagreement and future action to be taken. Once again, be wary of over-long, typed letters: they may give parents the impression that you are blaming them for what their child has done. It's often worth holding on to a draft overnight and reviewing it the next day. Even on a typed letter, I'm a great believer in the handwritten PS – including the one which makes a concession along the lines of: 'It's been a hectic day: I'm not sure that I have put all this very well, but please take this in the constructive spirit in which it's meant.' It will cost you nothing; it doesn't preclude any future options, and it may help the ongoing relationship with them.

Take a few notes while your memory is still strong – especially if anything unacceptable was thrown at you – just in case the parent decides to complain either informally or formally about how you handled the matter. Let your Head or deputy know if you think there is anything else your school can learn from your experience. Are there any procedures or routines that need to be reviewed? Think also in the days that follow about how you can pre-empt some aspects of future visits with their next problem. If their child makes a success of something in the next few weeks, fire off a message of congratulation: it will mean that you have goodwill in the bank when the next black clouds gather.

If the parents' relationship with a school (or a houseparent) is *fundamentally* good, in times of crisis they are more likely to draw positive conclusions when they first hear about a potential problem; if it isn't, those first impressions are more likely to be negative. So, if you have gone out of your way to educate your parents via (for example) such strategies as parental forums or guidance sheets on teenage parties, sleepovers, alcohol and illegal drugs; adolescence; uses and abuses of mobile phones and the internet; how to say 'no'; how to resist the notion that 'everyone else's parents let their children do it' *etc*, goodwill should have been accrued over time.

Above all, remind yourself that for every pair of Deeply-Concerneds there will be plenty of parents who are quietly and gratefully confident in the good work you are doing. Many years ago when I was under remorseless pressure from a group of parents, I received an anonymous item through the post. It contained some words from the philosopher, Edmund Burke (1729-97): 'Because half a dozen grasshoppers under a fern make the field ring with their importunate chink, while thousands of great cattle, reposed beneath the shadow of the British oak, chew the cud and are silent, pray do not imagine that those who make the noise are the only inhabitants of the field.'

I've kept it on a slip of paper in the letter-rack on my desk. From time to time it's been a great comfort. Good luck!

This chapter is based on two articles which first appeared in Conference & Common Room *in 2006. I am also very grateful to Emma McKendrick, Head of Downe House School, for permission to quote from her presentation to the BSA conference for housemasters and housemistresses in January 2008.*

Conclusion and Overview

Hilary Moriarty

Once upon a time, a Headteacher said to her young deputy, "The best pastoral care is a well taught curriculum." She didn't actually add, "Game over!", but if she had known the expression she probably would have used it, because I – the deputy in question – remember the remark as a conversation stopper. It brooked no argument.

And in a way, there *was* no argument: I knew she was referring to the importance of getting the actual content of the school day right for every pupil, though pupil-centred learning had not been invented then. If pupils were in the right classes, with the right peer group, and the right staff teaching the right subjects for the right examinations, all would be well, and all manner of things would be well.

At the time, I was worried about lunch breaks. An hour and a quarter in the middle of the day seemed to me perilous for many tender pupils, and downright dangerous for a few who were at risk of being teased or bullied behind the bike sheds. Did our pastoral care cover the time well? I found the then-novel continental idea of early starts and early finishes, with short, functional lunch breaks, very attractive. If the curriculum was really the answer to pastoral problems, pupils were better off in class than being let loose for too long.

"What about the hockey team?" said the Head.

"But that's at most 22 girls, and here are 400 other girls, with not enough to do – and they never take more than 20 minutes for lunch," said I.

"They should join the choir: that meets in two lunch times as well, and some girls are in the hockey team as well as the choir and it's important that they should have those opportunities."

Indeed it was. And the Head could have added – and probably did – that staff needed time to eat, as well as to conduct the choir, or blow whistles on the pitch. It's just possible words like 'tail', 'dog' and 'wag' might have entered my thoughts at this stage, but uttering them would have been a waste of time. I remember despairing at what seemed like another of those circles which schools were always trying to square; balancing the needs of this group against that; making allowance for the value of activities and the need for 'downtime'; wanting the day to be always purposeful, yet providing space for many talents to develop and protecting those who just might be at risk. In this particular case, there was clear reluctance to acknowledge that there might even be a problem, let alone to worry about how to deal with it.

At the time, there was certainly a presumption in many schools that their sole purpose was to teach. Anything else was incidental. My first brush with the very notion that pastoral care was important for its own sake was in a large, new comprehensive school being formed during reorganisation by the amalgamation of a grammar school and a secondary modern school. The Head of the new school decided that heads of academic departments would be on Scale 2, but heads of year, the pastoral equivalent, would be on Scale 3, and would thus earn more.

As a head of English with a Master's degree, I was incensed. It seemed to me that the school had declared an agenda which told academic staff, teaching examination classes, that they were worth less than their colleagues who seemed to be more concerned with supervising detentions and gathering information from the network of tutors. I protested.

The Headmaster chided me: "You do know how they are connected, the pastoral and the academic, don't you? In a school made up of two populations like this, with old enmities running deep, the year heads will have their work cut out for the next couple of years, making this one school, convincing children they can succeed in the new school. Your academic success depends on the work those pastoral heads will do."

He was probably right. Yet it still irked that they were paid more, and had lighter timetables because they needed to be available to trouble-shoot during the school day. As head of English, I had four free periods a week and did marking until midnight most nights. I left very soon afterwards, to take a similar post in a grammar school, where I still only had four free periods and I still marked until midnight – but at least I felt that the world was a fairer place, because year heads also had four free periods and earned no more than I did. I was still convinced the maths teachers had it easy, with their right or wrong answers and no 500 word essays from 30 pupils at a time, but that is a different story.

I feel I have lived in revolutionary times when I look back on these skirmishes with the very idea of pastoral care, and see how the world has turned. My Headmistress, who saw the curriculum as the magic wand to cure all ills, has been vindicated by the government insistence upon examinations as the ultimate barometer for schools. Is a school good or is it bad? Easy: check the exam scores and the number of A*-C passes; see the league tables; bingo. All is revealed.

Teachers would claim, and parents in their wiser moments know, that there is more to school than the scores on the doors, but there is a dreadful, seductive simplicity about numbers. They are memorable, quotable, succinct, sound-bitey and often irrefutable.

But they don't tell you the whole story. And they may not reveal the pastoral truth about a school. High grades may mean high pressure and stress, with serious outcomes.

Mercifully, and perhaps because they recognised the risks, the revolution in schools has encompassed enormous changes also in pastoral care. Nowadays our schools take it very seriously indeed, and not just because a happy child, well cared for, will achieve more than an unhappy youngster, struggling with stress or difficulty, academic or personal.

One of the outward manifestations of the new concern with pastoral care in schools is the development of what have become known as happiness classes. These are a product of psychological research which in recent times has branched out from the study of the abnormal in the human psyche, to delve deeply into the lessons to be learned from those – let us hope – many and happy people, who live long and live well. How do they do it? What do they have that people in the doldrums or who are just vaguely discontent do not? We are not so naive as to think that if we could find it we could bottle it, but surely we could all learn from such people?

If learning to be happy is possible, schools would be a very good place to teach it – and now many do just that. Experts in the field such as Nick Baylis have addressed conferences run by the Boarding Schools'

Association, leaving audiences buzzing with the intention to go back and do it better. That includes taking better care of themselves: "Remember when you were a child? What did you really want to do when you grew up? Are you doing it? If not, why not? And what could you do to get closer to that dream you started with?" Overheard in the corridor after that particular speech: "I'm going to call my husband tonight and tell him – I'm going to learn to ski!"

More important for the material explored in this small text, the intention to do it better was mostly directed to their young charges. Staff in schools today recognise the importance of real, honest to goodness, pastoral care for their pupils, over and above that expressed in the academic classroom and in the diligence of the quiet, silent marking of work. Pastoral care now goes further than the desultory: "You OK?" It really aims to make a difference to the lives our young charges lead.

If pastoral care has grown up in day schools, it has really come of age in the secluded world of boarding schools. If parents today are to trust us with their most precious child, for weeks at a time, we had better be good at the job and the job is a whole lot bigger than just getting the grades, important though that is.

How big a job it is, how diverse and how demanding, how responsible and how rewarding, how fascinating and how frustrating, is wonderfully well illustrated in these chapters. From the particular challenges of young boarders in prep schools to dealing with downright difficult teenagers; from the intricacies of a school nurse's world to observations on the role of the chaplain, colleagues offer us insight and honesty in their reflections.

They offer, also, and in large measure, their wisdom. It comes from years in their respective careers; practising what they now preach; moving with the times as they have themselves changed; making the all-round care of pupils in and out of the classroom their priority. They offer practical advice and philosophical reflection and, in a very real sense, food for thought.

My old Headmaster was right of course: the academic and pastoral concerns of schools do go hand in hand. The very fact that this is the longest in this series of volumes tells us much about the scale of interest in pastoral issues; the daily determination to do it right, in whatever role we have to play in the complex world of schools.

We hope you find it a useful point of reference and reassurance in the quiet moments of the busy term.

Afterword – an extract from *The Learning Game*

Jonathan Smith

Jonathan Smith taught English for many years at Tonbridge School. He has published six novels and written many plays for radio. His memoir, The Learning Game *(Little, Brown, 2000), became a bestseller and was* BBC Radio 4's Book of the Week.

We are very grateful to him for allowing us to reproduce the extract which follows. The detailed structures and administrative arrangements in education may change (for example, as coursework gives way to 'controlled assessments'), but the essential challenges – and the frailties that they reveal in those facing up to them – remain the same. This scene encapsulates many of the issues with which we all wrestle in providing effective pastoral care...

What is the thing most on the mind of sixteen-year-olds? According to the magazine I was reading in my hairdresser's the other day, it is sex – to which their minds and instincts return on average every thirty-seven seconds. A specially selected team has researched this in depth. They are wrong. It is not sex that obsesses many middle teenagers, though that flits in and out of focus. What obsesses them is another dreaded c word: course-work.

For four years running, from fifteen to eighteen, just when their emotional life is exploding, just when they are widely supposed and widely suspected to be experiencing for the first time the forbidden fruit, they are thinking about demands and pressures of an entirely different kind. In every classroom and on every corridor they are being told, 'Your English coursework is due in on Monday', 'The deadline for your geography project is Tuesday and any work handed in after that day WILL NOT COUNT', 'You are reminded that your drama coursework must be in by Wednesday at the latest (NO EXTENSIONS)', 'Your biology assessment...'

- Does it have to be in on Monday, sir?
- Yes.
- Sir!
- Monday I said, and Monday it is. I've said Monday a thousand times.
- I put mine under your door last Thursday.
- No, you didn't.
- I left it on your desk on Friday.
- No, you didn't.
- Can I hand it in tomorrow then?
- No, we all agreed Monday. We've been through all this!
- But my geography project is due in tomorrow.
- Tough.
- Yeah, but he goes ape if it's late, he really does.
- So do I.
- No, you don't, sir. He's scary, he won't budge, he never does... but you know what we're going through, you do, sir, you know how much we have to hand in. You're reasonable, sir. You don't think your subject is the only subject.
- Yes, I do.
- Not in the same way sir.
- It won't work, sorry.
- Is it a *real* deadline then, sir?
- What do you mean, 'a real deadline'?
- Matt Davies rang up the board, and they're not due in, the marks and folders, for another six weeks.
- The cheeky sod.
- So, what's all the rush?
- Well, that's the board's deadline, but we have an earlier deadline, all schools do, it's an internal matter. A departmental matter.
- Why?
- To do some moderation. We all sit down together, it takes hours, you've no idea. Comparing one class against another. Taking scripts from the top, middle and lower grades. Making sure we've got it right. Making sure you're all being treated absolutely fairly.

Applying the criteria. Believe it or not, we're professionals, and all this takes time.

- But you sit on our work for six weeks?
- Look, I'm not the head of department, get it in on Monday or else! Is that clear enough? Monday!
- There's another thing. I didn't want to tell you, sir, but I feel I should.
- Yes?
- Things aren't too good at home, sir.
- At home?
- They really aren't. I don't know how to tell you.
- Oh, I'm sorry to hear that... In what way?
- It's been getting to me. Everything. That's what's made me get behind.
- Look, I really am sorry, but I can't make exceptions.
- The thing is, my father's gone off with someone else a month ago, it's shattered my mum, I've never seen her like it, she doesn't know what's going on. And my sister's got anorexia.
- Gosh, that's, that's tough, that's difficult for you, I can see that. Even so, a deadline's a deadline. Your sister too... I'll have a word, I'll... see what I can do.
- Would you? Just till Friday, it'll be on your desk on Friday.
- I'll see what my colleagues say. I'll have to clear it with them. But no promises. OK?
- Thanks, sir, thanks a lot.

NOTES

NOTES

NOTES

NOTES